MW00715739

Only Paper, Merely Words

Shirley M. Wright Steinman

Bytesmiths Press • *www.Bytesmiths.com* • *West Linn, Oregon*

To
George
Jan
Gretchen
and Tim

Thank you for your encouragement

For My Children

I thought I could give you music
but I never learned how;
so the songs that sang in my head
disappeared, leaving

Only Paper
Merely Words

Just Four Ingredients

only paper
merely words
simply thoughts
nothing but feelings

do some measuring
blend or stir
simmer awhile
even stew
easy as pie
and no baking

but these four
can keep me awake
all night scribbling
arguing with my muse
crossing out
adding and erasing
reading aloud
tasting to see if any of this
is digestible

Contents

An Ordinary Woman • • • • • • • • 57

Tickle Your Funny Bone • • • • • 259

Forward

Only paper. Merely words. Simply understatement!

In a world where we act the way we're instructed, invest our personal resources according to what we see on TV, and elect our leaders according to how much money they've spent, contemplative thought seems to have fled to some safe crevice between Rationale and Excuse.

But contemplation alone is not what makes this book special. There are plenty of contemplators on the book circuit, hawking their wares on late–night TV, casting about for the perfect sound–bite, influencing opinion.

Now look around for humble contemplation. See any? Where is that Zen–like quality of thought beyond being? Where is the savoring of sweet, unavoidable pain, without blame or indignation? (Where is the indignation at avoidable pain!)

You're holding it in your hand.

Yet with this humility comes a form of hubris; not the pride of the stinking rich executive, taking the Fifth at a congressional hearing, not the smirk of the barely–literate dynastic politician, not even the blatant excess of the somewhat talented pop–star — but the satisfaction of knowing that there is the unknowable, and the joy of trying to describe it.

— Jan Steinman, 29 July 2002

Miracle and Mystery

In the Beginning, Mystery

We all somehow know that.
More than multi–gods
whose advocates reasoned:
How can so great talent and diversity
be the work of only one?
More than a One God for One People,
more, even, than that easy adoration
we feel when surrounded by
candles, choirs and stained glass.

Now we can see Black Holes.
We can see such an ever–expanding
Creativity, ever creating and then
recreating Itself, that at last, at long last,
we don't dare make It in our own poor image.
We dare not even woo It save in our role
as scientists, therefore fact–seekers.

If awe doesn't stop us cold for such
audacity, it's that we view It now
as a great Unknown that we'll make known.
We scorn those superstitious "pagans",
and even our own 2000 years
of putting Face and Name to It.

Still, In the beginning, Mystery.
In the end, Deeper Mystery.

Morning Exultation

Let's see what You brought me this morning,
O Magic of Magics!
Gossamer ribbons of spiderwebs traced by the dew.
Arachnids of uncounted thousands were summoned to spin them.
Then You woke me in time just to harvest the view.

What was it You gave to me yesterday,
O Worker of Wonders?
An orange–yellow brilliance is all I remember.
Oh yes, bittersweet cups opened wide by the frost of September.
As I feasted my eyes, I knew that the Giver was You.

What gift will you proffer tomorrow
O Dispeller of Dis–ease?
What gift to discover, bedazzle,
to play with, or simply to shine?
For this world's still all Yours
as you make it all, gradually, mine.

Each a Miracle

On fallow land
long waiting, but not wasting
diversity of seeds may find
each one its holy niches
and sing about its difference as it grows

Dressing

The sage is holy,
and the bread the staff of life.
When mixed and cooked,
they make the very thread
from me to those who came before.
They suffice for food
that fills me with thanksgiving
to be alive and be sustained
with the humble and the holy.

Contemplation in Sudden Sun

Dust motes
nonexistant mere moments ago
it seemed
are given life and form
by sun shaft.
My eyes blur to teary wonder.

Easy, now, to think Einstein's
light–quantum hypothesis:
light can act as particulate matter.
Easy, now, to hear the Man/God:
I Am the Way, the Truth, the Light.
Easy now that awe of the least
is teaching me preponderance of the Greatest.

Crystal

So there it is, then:
all living things and beings amid the dross
and the stink and the filth of their own decay.
And only the jewels and the crystals
wither not, nor fall down to rot.

Were they alive in some form once?
Was there breath and touch and motion?
Did they love and pity and take care of?
Did they withstand the fire
that led to their perfecting?

Does such logic predict that perseverance
in our small organic ways —
each fragile petalled bloom,
each wee flower of an infant's lifeline lips,
each pollen–heavy branch of tree —
leads but to permanence?

Christmas Again

Candle, Candle
Wreath, Wreath
Place the symbols of our longing
where they matter to our lives:
    at our windows
    on our tables
    pierced into our earlobes
    on the bumpers of our cars.

We wade into the turmoil of the crowd
to choose the costly trinkets for our clan,
then ease our conscience once again
by putting pennies in the pot as we emerge.

We wish again that we were better at it.
Hope again for some political miracle.
Wonder anew why we don't feed each hungry manger child.
Wish the world, and we, could find a better way,
find better answers somewhere in this boiling stew.

Candle, Candle
Wreath, Wreath
Work your ancient magic to transform our hearts
as we decorate this artificial tree
and wonder when the last real one will be gone.

Candle, Candle
Wreath, Wreath
Incantations against the mystery void.
Plumb our depths of fears and dreads.
Return us from that uninhabited terror
that we may not know or admit.
Then grant us peace and warmth and a wholeness
for the day.

Candle, Candle
Wreath, Wreath
Keep despair of having, or of not,
from hearts that need it for another year.
Let your voodoo charms protect us:
Candle, grant some light on darkest times.
Wreath, keep the circle of the People still intact.

Hope, After Watching "Threads"

When the music and the poetry went out
(and only incidentally, the lights),
The planet was an ugly, sterile, and an unforgiving thing.
God must have shrugged and turned away,
For we had finally fashioned Carson's Silent Spring.
Worse than any film could show, or scientist predict —
The blast, the firestorm, and the wind,
The freeze that followed close upon it all —
Far worse! For the men who took to caves for life,
So many of them already soul–sold nonfuturists,
Became mere louts, mechanically existing.

The food they labored for and coaxed to late fruition
Had flowers of no color and no smell.
The resultant foods were gross and tasteless lumps.
There was no leisure and no recreation,
Only sodden, listless coping, marked by snarling,
Smoldering tempers flaring up at random.
There were no flocks to watch, no pristine pastoral
Setting in which to nurture up a dreamer.
Necessity had buried sweet simplicity in nuclear dust.

Man had nearly lost his language,
For to fight his fellow for some snatch of pillaged offal,
Or to drape himself in rags or skins against the cold
Harsh grunts alone seemed to suffice.

It was to all of this that God turned back one day. He felt
Compassion melt His heart. He missed the rainbow
He had set as contract at that other time. He missed the way
That certain men had written and sung their gratitude.
Longing for the love of His createds filled His throat
And heaved His shoulders in a sob too great to bear.
And a tear fell down out of the eye of God and landed
On a lad at labor on the raped and unresponsive soil.
That tear of God so overwhelmed the boy, he dropped his stick,
And for the first time in his life raised up his eyes.
Fearful, hesitant, with joy and love and praise so new,
He sang one note and spoke one word for beauty's sake alone.
Thus man began again his daring, hopeful, painful phoenixing.

October Smokies
10–20–93

Not one lone standing splendor of fiery or gold leaf,
but avalanche upon avalanche
of soul–arresting beauty,
captured in my mind's best eye
what we had hoped to bring home with the camera.

That color, and that sun, those clouds, and that bright mood
made me quite giddy with recognition
that we stood in nature's own cathedral,
humbled by the majesty of stained–glass leaves.
Leaves, the rich embroidered tapestries on the walls.
Leaves, the oriental carpets that we stood on.

Friends and families, relatives and strangers,
all who looked partook together
of the sacrament of leaves.

Who's Even Tempted

to be bored must have a lot of nerve,
or arrogance,
or gross stupidity.
We're all given
words,
or signs,
or hues,
or sounds to play with.

We can contemplate for hours the clouds.
Or, if they're closed out,
the bars that keep us in,
or reasons why.
Can we not, then, dream
of freedoms by the lifetime,
or of free–breathing by the breath?

No one can steal our thoughts
of our lives past, or those
(for we're all alike sentenced)
of our up–coming deaths.
"I have nothing to do" is blasphemy.
"I'm bored" our only sin against life.

Christmas Again, II

The woman and the man,
 of sweet acquaintanceship,
Calming each other
 when the storms came,
Nourishing each other
 in the drought,
Soothing each other
 against the Big Fear,
Bringing forth life,
 when the world did not deserve it,

Watched their child
 as she balled her tiny fists
And squalled out her demands
 which were only: Love me,
For I am your love
 personified and magnified.
I am from a World
 you can't remember.
I am newly from such a One
 and such a Place. If you only knew!

So comes the Child to us
 with inexplicable faith
Each year anew, to wonder
 if we will accept,
And accepting, try to learn,
 and learning, try to change
The dross to silver. And if
 our best efforts only last
Until Good Friday, no one
 can better understand than He.

When, O Lord?

Why is it in those long times of waiting —
waiting for sleep
for the step of my love
for cessation of pain —
why is it then
that you come,
uncalled and unthought–of,
to speak and to show me,
direct or admonish or shame?

Why must I grope up or fall down,
or stumble in darkness,
afraid of your loss,
groggy dull with the waiting I've done,
afraid you'll not speak,
not repeat, not direct me,
afraid I'll not know you,
and fear that we two can't be one?

Talking to Potatoes in March

Blindly struggling like cave fish and lizard,
who once must have been eyed, like you,
before hopelessness took over for
an evolution of economy,
you seek and ever seek the Light.

I've come here often before into this dark
to snatch that hope you live with, and,
by this act, be the enabler of your freedom.
You can't know why; and I don't know if
those eyes weep anew each time.
But if I can keep you hopeful long enough,
you will regain the Light.

Cave bats, unlike the fish and lizards, have a knowing
of the upness on their side. You must be aware
of wanting that projection in your every cell
because you constantly start over when I have done
my worst. I wonder at your level of frustration
as you give again your very guts to live.

But, there now, I'll make a promise to you:
this is the last time, in this year, I'll take your
energy and faith and snap them off.
(I also ache for springs that do not come.)
I'll leave you now in peace until Good Friday's
planting starts you on a final upward climb
to what will be your newest Life.

Hope

Wedded to Hope,
I cannot give it up.
It was a vow I took, and willingly,
before I was aware despair existed.

A serious promise made
before the world and God.
Made when I was innocent and young.
I spoke my solemn and my white–veiled word.

May I step
into the crater of The Bomb
yet never faithless be?
Hope gave me this wedding ring. I wear it still.

Have I a choice?
Can dawn choose not to come?
Can trillium choose not to bloom in early spring?
Hope is my mate. I cannot hopeless be.

Grace Before

A record of my thankful list
(as if you didn't know):
arms flung out to welcome,
clarinet on upswing,
sun on leaf,
patch of red on black wing,
simultaneous sun with fiercest rainstorm,
and sunflowers at limp attention in a row.

Thanks for Cool Mornings

when the blankets snuggle up to me
and release me with reluctance

when long sleeves hug me clear
to the hands held in cup's embrace

when puffy quilts of fog tuck
all about me on the road

when the warmth of all the smiles
that greet me in the classroom

are put on and stop my shivering
enough to last till noon sun

takes over and does the job
with an unseasonal passion

then I throwing off my sweater
can pray appreciation for cool mornings

Thanksgiving

Let us celebrate
our very own personal feasts
and let them all be movable.
For seventy–five days, or years,
in a row, if need be,

we can dance and sing
with more harmony than the spheres,
for we will be one with Creation.
And if it takes a century
to recuperate enough
to celebrate again, Amen!

Let us answer to no one
at this moment, and keep
nothing holier than
the migrating geese.

Our lists of day's work to be done
and correctness to be spoken
are too long and barren
to be now celebrated.

For what is celebration but joy?
And each pebble of endless sand,
like Whitman's leaves of grass,
will be the range of our delight.

Lost and Found

I used to watch for spires once,
and search all clouds
when I was sky–dependent,
looking steeple–ward as if
those were the hills from
whence my help would come.

But now I only reverence
earthy things, like soil
beneath my feet, and those
unravelings of complicated
twinings of the plants.
The up has come to down,
the there to here.

I clamor for the now
of feet and mulch and
coverings of ground
as once I sought out God
in many high–up things.
False speech no longer calls,
and man–made tenets fail.

I know if reality exists,
it is the lore inside us,
rich, rich in histories,
in families, in kinds,
the loams of adoration.
If we find no love here,
then love (and God)
cannot be found at all.

For Sheila
July, 1998

Turning in slow, sunny circles,
feasting my eyes on all things held dear
(and all things are held dear),
I am trying to see them for you.

I'm held for full moments by the tower
of Golden Glow bloom. They smile like your
last, casket–smile. (O remarkable thing,
Sheila, your corpse with a grin!)
I'm willing that you see that too.
And you do! And you do!

I spoke to your flowers today,
in your back yard, when I'd told you good–by.
Then I just said hello again, my total belief
like the priest's, when he told us today,
"She did not die!"

The Visitation sisters fenceline was blue
with the bluest of chicory, your kind of blue.
I thought of you, rejoicing and knowing
that you see it too.

Released from your form's fetters
of time, distance and space,
You've now earned that enviable place
with your Pa, that's nowhere and everywhere
endless in grace.

From Sheila

August, 1998

My spirit speaks to everything that grows
My spirit ebbs, my spirit flows
My spirit weeps at sorrows that it knows
My spirit lifts off, and my spirit goes.

My spirit hungers for its own creator's breath
My spirit longs to know the length, the width, the breadth
My spirit calls out that such life will be its death
My spirit goes.

Let others weep when they cross eternal bands
I'll take this ship and sail those far–off lands
My spirit kens what my mind can't understand
It longs to reach those oh–so distant shores
My spirit soars!

Prayer

Help more powerless people become wise
Help more wise people become compassionate
Help more compassionate people gain more influence
over helping more powerless people

Amen

Real Loves, Real Lives

New Age

By courier I sent you a CD with my heart.
On it I'd typed all I knew of love and adoration.
You didn't answer.
The fax and modem sit forlorn
as I wish for kinder ages
in which I may have held your handkerchief
or tresses for my consolation.

Your old words flicker on the screen.
I may bring them back whenever I desire,
but the impersonal rigid plastic doesn't
smell like you. I may not hold it to my cheek.
May not take it up the darkened stairway
to my room and clutch it to my heart in sleep.

Enamor

My desire's not limited to lips
or hips or other protrusions of the torso.
The fine hair on your upper cheek
lit to white in the sun,
the soft inner flesh on your arm,
the dozens of crinkle curves that frame
and increase your warmth of eye —
these too are erotic.
The familiar scrawl on the note you leave
sets my pulse to racing
and my mind off in delicious fantasy.
Victoria's Secret doesn't know my secret:
each numbered freckle on your back
exists only for my kisses

The Door

What can I say we are,
My love and I?
Key and lock in infinite privacy,
But one–to–one;
Yet opening to the world
When we will.

For caring is that hinge
That closes in
When we are just for each;
Or swings about
To encompass everyone
When love has grown
Too great for this small room.

Coping

Sometimes I miss you with a shock
of bright intensity
like starflash.
Othertimes, a kind of tough and reasoned
close–to–accepting ache.

But there are days
when the missing turns quite stupid
and can't, or won't, be dealt with.

Then I run
(and I'm so unathletic)
or take a plane
(and I'm so afraid of flying)
not toward you —
I have at least bought
the truth of that finality —
but from the mingled joy and pain
all remembering you must be.

Love Song

I have seen you in the sun,
seen you incredible in brilliance,
walking toward me in your easy stride,
seeming unaware of all you cast in shade.

That star's rays burn into your now white hair,
force themselves into each dear crevice
of your familiar, aging face,
then cast back, as a prism, all that
gold and red and orange of your being.

I can only guess now how you'll look
standing in that other earthly light —
your body long and luminous and spiritual,
your colors of awake melting into sunset,
fading finally into the fastness of my dreams.

You are with me in mid–light now,
as any spirit must when it is but half–formed.
And we're each of us seeing darkly
through that glass of Paul's non–life.

But I will know your star.
I'll recognize those lines that I see here.
The glint and glare of you will not be lost
to me in times of timeless Time.

You are my love forever.

Dona Nobis Pacem

I can make peace with you,
if only those endearments spoke at night
can last this day's whole length for this one time.
Today's the problem, and its words.

We all are human things at night.
Our nestling, nurturing, harboring words, then,
hark to cave, to clan, to common roots that hold us.

Others, called in as arbiters,
won't stand a chance if we cannot retreat
from stubborn stances in the blaze of sun,
and both give way to evening and its calm.

"One day at a time",
muttered as mantra, stirs some deep well
of willingness to wait, and care about
what happens next, until it does;

for all wars (even ours, my love) are predicated
on the trust and pretense that no one guesses
that all peace is partial.

Missing

into that cave in the bed
beneath that comforting
comfortor's warm shield
I go to miss you

you've never been away
so long before
and the spot you sleep on's cold
too cold for comfort
not close
not anywhere near
comfortable

our cave is ice
and no amount of turning
up the thermostat
can warm it

My Phantom

He was an illusion of a man, not just of love.
Oh, he could grin!
And on some fading, yellowed
snapshot once, he did.
I remember grinning back
from the camera's eye,
not knowing yet the ghost I filmed.
A day of sun, an outing in fresh air,
a holiday don't bode of shades.

But that specter dogged me,
or betimes I chased him,
while my friends laughed at me
and pointed at their heads.

I still thought him real until
another picture–day when I touched him,
saw him dissolve beneath my hand
like mist in sudden sun.
When I developed that film,
there was no trace… except
a blurry, fuzzy smile without a face.

Those Three Words

Women want it said.
I have no doubt that tiny clause
must be the outset of the bane
of man's whole history
and the cause of the working strategy
of all his self–defense.

I suppose his mind works thus:
If I don't, I'm not responsible.
If I can't, then I'm available.
If I avoid it, I'm still accessible
in case of others stopping by.
If I do, I'll probably end up losing
all my rights to a roving eye.

But to us he says (having come but late
to this whole world of wrestling words),
that he shows us by his work.
He shows us by keeping (somewhat)
of a restraint upon that eye, and he
gives us things, too. Must he also give
away his freedom with the ironclad of words?

Being women, we persist in wanting
that small sentence. Being, from our history
born with craving of just one to make us whole,
need those words to rely on. We beg, without asking,
plead by the message in our eye. He's dense.
But we mustn't say it first. For if we do,
it doesn't count, because, forced out thus,
it's just an answer, not commitment.

Just Another Love Song

When ego rears its ugly head
to hammer down the sense of self in other,
we struggle for a meeting of the minds,
renewal of that one thing that we have
    Together.

When distance sorely aches our hearts,
and tortures naked arms with longing,
the constant pressure of each other's
spirit fans the flame of what we are
    Together.

When semblance of the real attacks
and lets the harsh world's things
into our private heart of being,
when explanations simply can't suffice
because they're based on that world's knowing,
then we will know just what we own
    Together.

Some count by tens, or millions,
and tally up their totals grand
with trumpetings of satisfaction.
We only have this simple sum
to keep all doubts and hateful words at bay:
we say, resay, then say again
that one and other one can still make one
    Together.

Grandma

Our world has failed to hold your attention.
You sit for those long, still countless hours
and stare unseeing at pale painted walls.
When they dress you, you are again an infant
and will not hold your arms up or your head.
The sleeve slipped over your hand stays unacknowledged.
When they feed you bites of the drab tasteless pap,
most times you will not swallow, and sometimes
grin impishly as the minced stuff passing for food
rolls back out from the corners of your mouth.

When they speak, voices over–bright,
needed contrast to the food, the walls,
you don't answer, but often flash a knowing smile.
They wash and comb you carefully,
like washing and combing a lifeless, lukewarm doll.
In tears they clip a ribbon to your sparse gray hair.

They visit you faithfully, guiltily, and talk to each other
about you, as though you already exist no more.
One sings to you softly about going home to Jesus.
One holds your hands for hours and silently weeps.
One can never quite look at you at all, but busies herself
tidying flowers and cards, finding fault with the food and the cleaning.
Years drag past with few signs from you that you're here.
At holidays they cover a small board with tinsel and cards
while your eyes seek only the same blank wall.

Grandma, to what lovely fields of flowers and sun
has your mind chosen to transport you?
What memories flood your being with such meaning
that they hold you to the past
from those who call you to the present?
What adventure are you on in your mind
that is so much livelier than any we can offer?

For My Mother
Edna Irene Paige Wright
April 2002

She would return now as she aged,
time and time anew, to her mother's wisdom.

Her father had left her such rich gifts:
fierce loyalty to good unions,
rejection of all racism,
the dignity of having little.

But her mother gave her feelings,
gave her mantras of the heart.
Taught her how to look at nature,
freely, closely, always grateful.
Taught her life was innocent and fragile,
that you can't kill it and still love it.
Taught her that all wars are evil,
that growth of large must never crush the small.
Taught that freedom is an inner thing
that never can be vanquished.
Taught her the rapture that is living right.
Taught her Quaker quiet, and a peace inside
while all the world outside is raging.
Taught her she had many cheeks to turn.

She turned them now (the darkest time she'd known),
and sat, and drew upon her mother's calm.

John N. Wright

My Daddy was a union man
AF of L
He told me of the viaduct
Said he saw the policemen
deliberately breaking knees
of the strikers
Told me of an outraged sense of justice
Taught me his fairness
So I learned early on
that the "right" of protest is a Duty

My Daddy was a news and sports man
I never picked up on the sports part
except the only reason I can
fill in the names of old Tigers
in the crosswords is due to
those names drumming themselves
into the ears of my childhood

My Daddy had the ability
still to me irrational
to simultaneously read the sports page
listen to a game on the radio
by means of a plug into his ear
and watch a different game on TV

My Daddy into his eighties
still read three newspapers daily
Taught me to always "keep up"
Never referred to Reagan except
to say, "He's only an acting president"

My Daddy was a fisherman
I was 21 and he helped me pick out
my very first car, then took time
every day for a while to teach
me to drive in Detroit traffic
Took me to a lake near Plymouth
to learn how to fish
I didn't like catching them
smelling them
cleaning them
or eating them
But I liked to row the boat
and to be there while my Daddy
tried to teach me fishing

Garage Sale

We spent the year
collecting stuff to sell.
We said, "When spring finally breaks,
we'll set the lot outdoors
and advertise. Then this old junk
will be someone else's prize."

But as we looked, and dusted off
each piece to judge and price,
a thing or two would catch our eye
(or heart), and we'd remember
when Dad last used that fishing rod,
or that the fluted blue candy dish
was Mother's very favorite.

We'd have to take the thing back in
and keep it still. It was too close,
touched us too near our core,
spoke to us of a time we wished
had not passed on —
as now our parents had.

Sisters
for Barb

I shall undoubtedly stay awake with you,
when you visit, until the day.
And we'll talk calmly then, and candidly,
perhaps of the way we were raised,
or how we raised our own,
or how our children are raising theirs.
Some politics, perhaps, some religion,
some tale of a friend enter in.

So we'll talk, and we'll laugh quite a lot
over, maybe, toast or buttered popcorn.
We'll stay reasonably awake the whole time
(though waves of sleep may try to engulf us),
with strong, hot, black coffee.
(though I like mine sweetened, with cream,
and you, since your ulcers, shouldn't drink it at all.)

There can't be a third person present,
not a child, or a husband, or grandchild.
If one intrudes, then we must start over this ritual,
begun somewhere in long ago childhood.
A ritual shutting out those who cannot understand,
the ritual of our very relationship, limited
by its unique own name to just us.
This ritual a gift from our mother.
Mother who showed us that sisters,
after separation of mere months or long years,
must stay up all night and just talk.

The Closet Humanitarian
for Dick

He would probably hate to think
that someone had outed him,
even after death.

He wasn't rich,
yet seemed to buy the rich's
arguments against the poor,
and ranted loudly on
about lack of responsibility.
Even financial responsibility,
but only when the poor were guilty
of unwise spending of their pennies.
Wore blinders to the well–off's
waste and hoarding of their millions.
Would not entertain the theory
that those millions had been amassed
through systematic robbing of the poor.
Called me, and others if they broached
the thought, foolish Bleeding Hearts.

He seemed to think that
blacks, Latinos, and the general poor
stole personally from him
when they cried out for
or dared to snatch some of the crumbs
that fell from off the rich men's tables.
Any legislation that came down
doling out, or even threatening to dole,
help to the helpless was anathema.

Yet this man was color–blind and kind
when little kids were cold.
Those kids who had to learn
to read and write (the language of the
Official English people, not their own)
with their coats and gloves on;
and his sense of justice knew
this should not be.
So he purchased them a furnace.

He was willing to spend his hard–earned cash
(for he'd always been in the working class)
to consistently help calm the hunger
of others' unwanted dogs, and a stray
could find comfort and ease
inside his home 'til he found it another.
He often put real food
in the homes of the very real poor,
and breathed not a word of it.

El hombre grande sin chaqueta
the locals called him,
and who knows now if someone shivers
less inside that Big Man's coat?

Now we're left here to wonder:
what other brash, brave acts
did this humanitarian do
that would belie his words?

To My Newborn

Were you made like the single
creative chemical grandeur
that could form a crystal —
     one second nothing,
     the next full–formed,
     hardened to perfection
     and clean–cut brilliance?

Is the soul of you,
that perfect, perfect core,
planted in forevermoreness,
     yet,
in one small destructible vessel,
just split–moments away
from being quite another person?

So vulnerable you lie,
sucking, sucking in sleep.
     There can be no better me
     than the parent who looks down
     now, filled with total awe,
     at you and your beginning.

You and I must both remember,
if some future confrontation rends us,
that you will always be Creation's best;
and I will stay as today:
proud and humble procreator.

New Potatoes

for Gretchen

No crust has formed yet,
no winter protective skin,
no hardened exterior.
So my knife skims without effort
over the tender surface,
drawing off the earth–brown newness,
preserving all those wondrous nutrients
found so close to the skin.

The little one crawling over the floor
cannot yet walk, but grabs my leg
with a fierce determination and pulls
herself with shouts of accomplishment
to wobbly legs, then plants herself beside me.

Soon her unsure legs, lacking strength for long,
give way. She lands, her little face showing
one part surprise, one part sheer grit.
She crawls away then back again to repeat
the standing maneuver over and over.

I weep for her unblemished perfection,
for the bruises she is going to collect,
for the exquisite delicacy of her skin,
but most for the tough shell that may replace it.

They Call It Parenthood

Trust, a fragile butterfly
With tissue paper wings.
I saw it in a child's eyes
And in the upraised hand
It offered me.

Much, much later, after:
    Bible stories
    vitamins
    seatbelts
    kissed hurts
Bundle–up–snowsuits
    Library cards
    Homework help
    Fevered heads
    Chickenpox
    Mended tears
Holding–after–nightmares
    Bike balancing
    Endless practice
    Proud recitals
    Buried kittens
    Quieted fears
Rainy–camping–trips
    Shared giggles
    High heels
    Driver's license
    Telephone calls
    Important Peers
And braces–off–teeth,
I watched the delicate wings lift
And flutter, and fly away,
Without once glancing back.
But I'll wait.

Wet Mothers Day

I did not warrant their lauds
on this day when I'd been nothing
save natural, just myself,
no attempt at that ideal other.

Their greetings were for that
perfect wonder I was not;
their tenderness drew a veil
down over old animosities;
their caring words erased
all that bitter past pettiness.

I stood to see them leave
in rain–soaked clothes to ride
the hearse of what knowing brings.

I longed to cry out, "I'd save you,
if I could, from these and later tears,"
but I know too well how salt cleanses.

Little February Filly
for Kara
February 25, 1996

Your mother and your father
who gave your soul a body
were children of the winter.

December, January, February,
harsh triumvirate of cold,
yet each brought the wonder
of a baby born to warm its parents' hearts.

Winter can no longer threaten,
last too long, or be too cold
if captured by sweet baby's smile
or looked at through a blessed newborn's eyes.

No Sweat

She felt so minimal she wept.
Not much had happened
on the outside.
He had not left her
when she feared he might.
She had not died
that time she came so close.
Their children hadn't failed
to rise up from their falls.
The nuclear plant, so far, not melted down.

Yet all that worry of the near–events,
the prayers, the fears, the dreads
had left her lined and feeling scarred.
Each assault upon her faith
had etched her face anew.
Even her short, stout stature
felt unequal to the task of hoping more.
Yet, "You've had an easy life," they told her.
She nodded then, and gave a wrinkled grin,
"Oh, yes!" she agreed with them, "I have!"

Depths of Understanding

He cared about his journey
into technology.
It was a way he could explain Grace.

Some see light
and bless the lantern–holder.
Some see light
and explain it with
amps, lumens and speeds
and think they know it better.

For J. M.

Your hands are soft, gentle, very smooth,
smooth as the wash of your accent.
I will never see your land, your India,
never know what ages of caste have done,
never realize the why of the revulsion
that brings pain to your kind voice.

This country's newer, its caste system's
only centuries old. I watch your mind
willing to dismiss as fixable the problems
your country's so long held to its proud heart.
As always, you gauge us on a different scale.

Traditions of your own (are we really too young
for our own traditions?) take you smiling back;
but changes here, and the fools' hopes,
force you to return here to compare.
I wish we could be as gentle on your faith
as your hands and voice are on us.

Frank Kuron
My Commissioner
October 29, 1997

Frank never bowed to expediency,
which can be threatening
to both the well–oiled and to the oiler.
He held no pretty masks
before his honest, earnest face.

Rough–voiced man of tender heart,
asking simply justice,
demanding purely truth,
we will miss you; all of us will,
for even the Suits are intelligent enough
to miss their formidable adversary.
You were on to them, and told them so
in all your valiant, sometimes vain, efforts
to bring facts to the harsh light of day.

All the aged and handicapped souls
at the county home will remember
that you fought for their birthday cakes.
That young man, filthy and sick on the street,
will remember you fought for his dignity.
And all of us pleased to be your constituents
will never forget your bright voice on the phone:
"Hello! Frank Kuron, Your Commissioner!"

The Magic

Come play, again, the elf for Christmas.
You know you always want to.
Practice up on your Ho's and shake that
too–stuffed belly before the mirror.

Paste those white brows atop your great dark bushes.
Pat that silky, shiny beard in place, just so.
Pull on your tall black boots, and sit amid
that fake snow with awe–struck youngsters
on your knees while you breathe out benevolence
and breathe in your greatest annual joy.

You never could quit believing in it,
could you? You always cut and trimmed
the tree and prayed for snow. You hung
those blasted lights, so many and so bright
I'm sure they kept the neighbors up at night.
Your whole bonus check at times
was thrown into one long holiday of hope
that began too early (though of course
you never asked me) and carried on for
far too long. And try my damnedest, all those
years I never heard the angel's song; still
you believed, and dragged or pushed
the rest of us along with you.

And now, our children gone, and friends
of former times moved far away, I'd just
as soon forget the day, and treat it as the
monstrous waste it is, but, as always, you persist.
Don't think I didn't see you when you
circled that small ad. It's one you never
did before: Santa in the window of a store.
I'll come and see you, though, and realize
the whole thing's not for show. I'll watch
the magic you believe in jump from your dear
eyes to light another's, and not curse my lot.

To be the wife of one who still believes
is not the cruelest of fates, as I so long have
thought. You live upon that magic which,
if left to me, would long have been forgot.

Our Friend Bert

She avoided facing feelings
for honest feelings hurt.
Blythe Pollyanna of the written word,
she couldn't, wouldn't, dared not
write of pain, or even think about
her non–admission.

Better to just avoid the deep–hid senses
(save for those initials she could not ignore,
still afraid to spell the whole words and their hurt)
and write of simple happiness
as though that's all there is.

Keep it light, with no tears, no frowns,
no punishments, and no retribution.
And change the subject fast
if someone else forgets.

Her feelings and creative gifts
now blocked by pain:
    pain of friendship's end,
    pain of health's retreat,
    pain of thoughts that will not let her sleep.
Huddling here, she suffers loss
while denying how her loss affects her.

Bert dear, you fail to realize that
we all are wounded in our struggles here,
and that wounds acknowledged
are the first to bleed and cleanse themselves,
then heal.

To My Friend

The cottonwood fluffs blew all about us on that day,
and they tickled our noses and we laughed with abandon.
Then something you said made me start to giggle.
I repeated it and you giggled too, and we just couldn't stop.

Like a reprieve came from being adults on that day.
Freedom came from thinking adult thoughts.
The gift that we gave to each other on that day in June
was all the freedom of childhood *that close* to being forgotten.

Not since a little girl in church had I found myself
caught so in the throes of giggles like these.
A female thing, I think, for only my closest girlfriends
and I had ever been mutually locked into them like this.

The next day my face ached with the imprint, still there,
of muscles contorted by unhabitual laughter.
I've never had a drinking buddy, never cared to drink.
But the next time that this world's pressures
get too brutal to handle, I'll know that it's time
to find you again, to seek out my giggling friend.

Winter Scene

The empty three–pony miniature
Merry–Go–Round in front of the
grocery turned to the tune of
the Beer Barrel Polka
as the old woman fed it coins.
The wind whipped the tinny tune
faintly into the night's coldness.

She wore neither hat nor gloves,
and her long white hair blew wildly
over her lined, smile–lit face.
She clapped and tapped her foot
with the music, frequently waving
and blowing kisses to invisible children.

Finally the last turn and song
were done, as the small change purse
had emptied to nothingness.
The old one gave a giant sigh,
sat down on the curb in the snow,
and cried for the children who weren't.

Good–by Sorrow

We crossed some undetermined ground
there could be no retreating from
when we each acknowledged grief.
Each had an open wound to deal with.
Each stood helpless at stemming his own flow.
Neither could glibly say he'd known
such loss before, nor could we emerge enough
from weeping to analyze why we were
each drawn so to the other.

There never had been desolate as this.
Not in the whole time and space continuum such sorrow.
So we two held on there together to honor
these, our losses. Then (miracle, we thought)
the souls' aches became the bodies',
and we meshed, believing for the time
a hole had thus been filled and satisfied.

We became time travelers, each submitting
pain to each to fuel the journey. We swore
we merely sought abatement of the hurt,
not a new and different intermingling of pain.
That's all I share with you. I hesitate to say
that it's not enough; some relationships share less.
But to merely be a part of loss is to be less
than life demands. I hope you see this too.

May you remember us as that whole
that once kept each others' sanity.

Waste

I knew a boy of quite stupendous power.
He had a ready laugh, a quick and steady wit.
He had an ease of manner, rare in children
He could have done such things
had he but put his talents to it.

He had a charming way with him,
and I admit I never could be strict —
he smiled too well at all of us.
True it is that I did sometimes rue
such mediocre output from so fine a mind
as his, but I was tolerant, just begged
he not be bored with average fare, but go
beyond and rise to meet a challenge.
It isn't that I let, or pushed for him to, lead.
Some boys are ever at the front of all the lines;
just, perhaps, as some must always follow.
And a host of ten–year–olds lined up behind
this boy. That's how it was.

We all knew about his broken home;
school records keep accounts so flat and cold,
we never do find half the truth in them.
I have grown far too old to seek a memory–
passage back to then for very long.
I only know that he captured me complete.
But a teacher's captive of at least a child a year,
and I fear I quietly just took note of his passing.
I was secure in knowing he was a leader,
and that someday I would read of him.

I read of him just six years from that day;
he'd got a gun and blown his head away.
I knew that wonderful child when he was ten.
I never saw him or his sweet promise again.

An Ordinary Woman

Autobiographical Note

The niche I fit in
is so low
so small
so hidden–close–to–ground
you must lower yourself
to see it,
get dirt on your knees
to talk to me.
Most of you will never
even know I'm here.
But I found it;
I fit it comfortably,
and it's mine.

The Joining

Contemplating verve and skill:
One says, "I can."
One says, "I will!"

When chance acts to combine the two,
The new element shouts out,
"I do! I do!"

I Shall Keep

I shall keep in this small space the right to it.
This prison cell a very den of liberty!
What evolved to me of thought, of cunning, and of peace
(when masses screamed for moment and their rights;
and "ethnic cleansing" proved them all unclean)
left this minuscule spot empty on life's wall.

As a barnacle or slipper shell moves to fill its inch's fraction,
with its own right to breathe, so I found this piece of freedom
all unspoken for, then claimed it mine without a flag.
I bask here in it, while all of you outside,
who cannot hear my words, think my lips move in silence.
Or that the tininess of my confinement somehow
gives you more freedom, space, or voice than I.

Worry Stone

The stone takes my worry as I rub
and dissolves it into nothingness.
The circle is complete,
for I brought this anxiety
from out the cores of lack of trust
and lack of vision, which are,
in essence, nil.

My stone just fits my thumb
which I had placed against my nose
in rash derision of unknowing.
Such arrogance pulses down the arm
from heart and mind and into a hand
that held the anger of a fist
just wistfulness ago.

Why worry then?
Just for having cares fall into nothing.

Seeing Old Ruins, Hearing Old Flutes

When my eye catches that ancient arch,
I congratulate myself.
If my being can recognize such beauty,
am I not also architect and builder–up of it?

Unity of spirit cries up
from the Indian flute to my heart's core,
plucks melody from a wave of sound
that would have engulfed me, stifled me
had I not opened to it,
had I not recognized the value of the other
in us all, had not wanted willing oneness.

Now we are together —
ancient arch and flute and I.
We form a fused whole, a timeless caring
for each other, and for
creator, creation, created.
Thus we join with all gods,
formed, formless, now forming.

Triplets

The norm is two,
which she'd surpassed by half.
I found the least one first,
shivering and wet.
She was so small and frail
as I rubbed her with a towel.
Later we saw the other two,
robust and strong,
with the puzzled mother.
Three kids to feed with just two feeders.

As the weeks passed,
we watched her butted out, the runt.
She tried to nurse, and the mother pulled away.
She put her head up to the feedbox,
and was pushed aside by stronger siblings.
Perhaps some natural law
of fitness and surviving.

But I'm a proud defier
of the unfair laws of life.
If it isn't just, then I just won't accept it.
So the mother has her twins,
and I've a little doe to bottle–feed.

The Owl

I had the chance
When the blackbird called
To stir myself,
Break–of–day and stuff,
That new beginning.
But I lolled in bed,
Or listlessly arose
To taste a stagnant day.

I felt a twinge
When the robin chirped
The rainy noontime through.
I just might get a move on,
But I munched dry toast,
And lazily stretched,
And slowly thought out, "Later."

My senses quivered
When the mourning dove
In dusky gray
Sighed her evening sigh
From the evergreens.
I thought to put my brain in gear,
But it chugged in first,
And only made me yawn.

But now at midnight hour
The clock's gone round
To a lovely time.
The stars are showing off.
The town lies sleeping.
And I am here, awake, alive, alert,
And filled with sweet ambition.

Of Beginnings

Gradually, gradually learning.
(Education's not just for the swift.)
I walk slow; I speak soft;
I ken little; yet I feel that I grow.

Gradually, gradually, like just one
of the trillions of seeds in an inch of the loam,
I'm stretching toward truth, and attaining
some tiny snatch of it here, or a whiff
of it there, borne to me, imperceptively, on the air.

Will I die before what I'm allotted
implodes with a sureness within?
Will I help any others who stretch by my side?
Lift them up? Hold their hands?
Point their eyes in direction of light?
I don't know. I just know that I grow.

Conciliation

Sweet and lukewarm coffee
filling up some void in my today,
I sit and sip and think.
I realize now I've carried
bitter memories on my back
and in my craw too long.

I bought into blaming
and disclaiming, and lost
the argument at last
because I chose to argue.

No fight / no losers
I've discovered.
I now must desperately, respectfully seek
to keep from battle,
pitying the oppressors now as well,
where once I pitied only the oppressed.

Puzzling It Out

I cut myself into large pieces that could
float into some bleak dawn which
I couldn't swim.

But when each piece achieved
the place I sought, it appeared
without its puzzle mates
and faded shyly into background.

So learn to swim.
Don't let tide or current merely
plot your destiny.
And stay in one whole entity.

It is impossible to guard all doors,
to see all auras,
though a wretched piece of you is yearning.

But it just may be possible
to see a subject whole,
and to be in one place entire
and undistraught by multiples.

No big deal to come in second
in a race you didn't know you'd entered,
just that you reach your goal intact.

October Musing

The garden's past,
gone down to defeat
beneath the hordes of marching weeds,
relentless, pushy, greedy,
who always conquer all.

Poor Calaban, stray cat,
meows a mournful dirge,
trying to follow me
as I collect the meager
harvest left to us:
tomato here, green pepper there,
a handful of dried beans
for one last small pot of soup.

Cool nights, emotionless,
pointing up wet mornings.
Patchy fog pulling a fluffy coverlet
over the garden dead.

Check the woodpile now
'gainst winter's thrust.
Pick the last pear.
Squeeze the apple's life
for sipping hot with cinnamon
around the friendly stove.

Nears the time
for viewing of old pictures,
for counting our remembers,
for crocheting by the lamp.

Come Calaban, don't cry.
Come join our hibernation.
Our pulses slow;
our heads nod over our tea;
and you can curl, a contented ball,
before the fire.

Unreason

I'm tired of this role now;
I want it to stop.
I don't want to be leader,
just some breath at the top.

Let me make decisions now.
My turn to be... well, surely not boss;
but I do have some opinions
I don't want you to cross.

I know we had an agreement,
but I didn't know
that I'd be so depressed here
with no room to grow.

It's not always great on the bottom, you'll find.
No good as just body, no soul and no mind.
No fun to stare way up at you till I'm blind.
I just can't fit in this space you defined.

Let me up!
Let me move!
Let me be!
Let me prove, if I can,
When the vote's in
that it's no sin
if you don't win
just because you're a man!

Most Common Decency

He rushed to hold the door for me,
but I would not go.
I would not buy obeisance.
Would not sit there in the age–old woman's chair.

I was neither better
nor less than he
because our sex was not the same,
no more worthy of preceding
because he, male,
had made a gesture for a female, me.

I felt rude, and he looked hurt,
or at least confused.
We'd gone and changed the rules
that he'd been raised with.
But for our daughters and our sons
it has to be, so they can learn
to go through doors together.

Male Order

If you forbid me, that's your problem.
As easily forbid the forming of a fist,
as easily tell God you don't care for Its commandments,
or the sea, its tide.

Must–be–obeyed days are just now over;
You should read the papers, or watch Oprah.
Does Man's unlearning have as far to go
as Woman's? Or are we still, even on
that question, far from equal?

Scales from the Eyes

Back there
hidden in endless aeons,
truth rode the dust of history.
Not commanding
(as it had every right),
but respecting differences
and waiting for discoveries,
it rode in silence.

The excellence of its mandate
is that it leaves to each to find,
in his or her or its own way,
(and achingly own time),
the inescapable WHO and WHAT
of all creation and all reason.

It still haunts and follows us.
Riding on that dust of uselessness
and rust, of glory or of meaningless remorse.
It still calls to us, marks well our decisions.
It writes us up in its eternal file,
but not as winners or losers,
just notes of us how well or ill,
how just or how unfair;
then totals up
how far we may have come,
or how far yet to go.

To Speak of It

Were there any other way to tell,
I would not speak.
If touch, or glance, or motion of the hand alone
could send my message out,
I'd not attempt to craft in words.

For all we vainly brag our language skill,
the other animals found a better way.
Words can be so harsh, the meaning of them
fallen off from flesh and breath and smile,
and other God–like attributes, that without great care
a coldness, a rigidity sets in. I, for one, dread
the use of tongue and teeth to say,
and even of the hand to pen, what may not be
the very it my being longs to send.

Still, and knowing this, I will withhold now
from you everything, save words.
We'll see if any remnants still are living love.
After the letter and the speech, will my prayer be wordless?
With only love words can my entity be prayer?

If You Write

If you write fiction,
you may deal with all emotions:
selfishness, love, hate, greed, passion.
In your people's lives you can do anything,
create any world, tell of any human foible,
climb any heights, achieve any dream.
And you don't have to answer for them,
not do time for them, not apologize.
Even if they make you weep,
it's all pretend. The moral stands.

If you write nonfiction,
you may plumb the depths of knowledge
and then teach. You may hold power
in your words that sway opinion, or that
move political action or develop conscience.
You may enlighten in a way that's not
been thought out before, may present a view
or thoughts that others hadn't accessed.

If you write poetry,
you can stretch your heart to anyone's
alive or dead, compact the rhythm of life
into the confines of brief lines. You may
create word–flowers remembered, smelled,
long after you yourself have gone away.

Then you find the beings you have made,
situations, characteristics you've created,
rhythms you have played with, logic you
have given life to, all fight with your senses,
won't let you sleep, scream for your attention,
invade your smallest bit of privacy.

To write is to be owned by your own words.

The Power

I enter the book composed.
I'm cool and determined, but indifferent at first.
The colored cover has gently drawn me in.
It is new genre.

I am entranced.
Hours later I emerge,
sweaty, shaken,
experienced.
Writers should not be allowed to entrap so
without warning.

Later, I cannot sleep,
but am haunted by a world I knew not,
yet have lived,
through the penmarks of someone else's mind.

Soft Voice of a Fat Bookworm

I am that constant rudder, set in one direction,
heading me ever inward, toward my own shore.
I never really longed to see another.

I study all those maps that others made,
look at pictures of our precious planet from space,
see woods and glens, mountains and oceans
that others visited and wrote about,
sopping like a sponge of all my eyes can read,
both foolishness and wisdom.
I ruminate, digest, hold counsel with myself,
then decide for me where I must stand.

Home in this warm den, and lost in books,
I've seen and been, immersed myself in others'
impressions, figured out the world with my affections.

They Are Not Ours

It was not my image,
though I'd thought it mine.
I put it on and wore it
like a barely worn sweater
from a secondhand store.
I loved it so, wore it so much,
it took on the shape of me.

One day I met a poet,
wearing my sweater, but so
different in color, the cut
not quite the same, and his
form had made it his.
I wondered then if I or he
should own this set of
telling words. He'd woven
his to plaid; mine a softer
nap and of pastel hue.
Are we both the author?

So we must speak to each
in this and every learning age
whatever they would love,
appreciate, or want to hear.
And if we're wise we realize
in the end we each own nothing.

We only stand with help from those before us.
We only walk on paths that others formed.

Experiment with Conceit
Upon Reading Sir Thomas Wyatt

Love, as a storm, held off and would not hit.
I told him of my plight, the needy bit
of flowers dying for the lack of it,
how the aged, cracked ground (my knowledge and my wit)
could persevere no longer in the game.
The garden would be lost, and all the same

to Love, for he sought that weed, my heart, to tame.
I wished him there, yet blushed at my bold shame.
Then sudden light and frenzied flood did rush at me
and tried to wash my garden to the sea.
I needed time to think, and drink this gust
of love, but he struck, and as soon deserted me.

Damn the rages of intoxicating Love
that I am left the worse for sipping of!

Da–Da, Da–Da

Rhymed lines lurch out to assault me when I'm walking,
Picking up the tramp and the half–step beat.
Insert themselves between us when we're talking;
Wave out to me from windows on the street.

If they would ever stop their insane chatter,
I'd likely find me better things to do.
I'd concentrate on things that really matter,
actually do a worthwhile deed or two.

But the rhymes and meters will not cease their flaying.
With my ears and mind and heart they do their will.
Even when I'm kneeling, rapt in praying,
Hands over ears, I hear those damned pests still!

So not cured yet, just endured must be my betting.
Can't beat 'em, I must join 'em in their fun.
I'll write them down, then quick! on to forgetting.
For, once scribbled out, they're for the moment done.

Strays

Poems knock upon my mind,
and I refuse them entrance.
Cowardly, I hide behind the
drapings at the window and look out.
There's too much pain in feeling,
too much effort raising the poor,
fatherless poems all alone.
Isn't there a national Poem–Care Plan?
A shelter for homeless poems?
A Muse–Catcher I can call?

The kitten stretches its paw beneath
the door to touch my unshod feet.
I laugh in relief at a thing so young,
so soft, and wanting only contact,
nothing more (until the food bowl's empty),
nothing more than curling on my lap
when sleepy, nothing more than the imprint
on my mind of its perfection.
I open the door wide, and widely smile
as poems and cat come tumbling in together.

Book Chant

Someone to talk to, not with.
Out of compulsive need to express
to another my joys, and my hates,
and the sums of my dreams, nothing less,
someone to talk to, not with.

And readers will be those wise someones,
their smiles and their nods sweeping
page after page of the text. But all their
brave, blustery rebuttals lost to me
in the swish of a leaf faded to history —
for I merely speak to them, not with.

Then they, in their turn, writing down
all they learned (if only a pollen–sized
dust–speck) from me, will mix it
and blend it, and add their own dash,
(just a splash of rare herb it may be).

But they'll send it out then to a new
crop of readers, come forth with admixtures
of grace and good sense, who will read
then agree, or dismiss, or catch on,
then write it all down to someone, not with.

If Ever

Will I do it, if my time is long enough,
finish those fits and starts
I've scribbled through the years
on backs of envelopes, on shopping lists,
on junk mail, on old bills and calendars?
Like Hansel and Gretel and the bread crumbs
will they lead somewhere, give one clue
to anyone of who I am and was, or just
be eaten up by birds, or tossed in a landfill?

If I have time, will I complete
that labor after inspiration's past:
the dictionary, counted beat,
Roget's confirmation? Or will I
know only my own mind's content,
that thus I have been made and formed?
Anything more may just be stolen time,
and a begging of God's patience.

My Calendar

All things are slanted on my calendar.
I write with it on the wall, and there it stays.
I cannot tip it back again
like writing at a table,
cannot make them straight again,
my slanted plans,
my tipped abbreviations for the future.

So I see them as I wrote,
leaning oh–so left.
And so I lean,
not really wanting any other way
but as my heart sees.
Things I must do tomorrow,
plans I may never keep,
resolutions that have formed me
through my left–turned eyes.
All things, joyfully, slant me for my day,
for left is where my heart is.

Old Stoves, Old People

She was feeling temporary
the day they bought the stove.
She'd reached some random
number in the aging years
so that she looked up, at the ready,
every time the doorbell rang
to see if death approached,
or at least his final illness.

She'd got to glancing at the obits
differently, not just the brief
daily prayer she'd long sent up.
Now she looked at ages.
Appalled, the days she saw the numbers
smaller than her own. Dare–to–hope
on days when all the years were more.
Not yet, dark angel, still not yet.

She needed a stove, a range to cook on.
They'd finally quit burning wood for that,
and the old electric one was rusted through.
She felt ashamed to spend on such a thing,
her years now clearly numbered; so she'd
chosen easily, by the price tag: cheapest.
No gadgets, though she'd miss the timer.

Now some way, though prayers and obits
still were noted, she'd made it ten more years.
The cheap, thin steel had rusted, and chips
in the thin porcelain marred the edges
of the ruined burner rings. No way to scour
it out. She couldn't clean it up.

Life lasts longer than you think it may.
Better buy that more expensive stove.

Past Tensing

I heard a ringing in my ears of yestertime,
a yen for older buildings, fashions, harsher climes,
of summers sweet with blessings,
of winters harsh with stings.
I had a longing for a thousand lesser things
than this now–world offers.
I had a yearning for dead innocence
and faith in happy endings
that had eroded into dust around my feet,
that dust the only food I found to eat.

It's not that I had seen it all.
I had no blasé problems. Merely thinking
on the past left me no time for boredom.
It was only the lack of simple satisfaction
with the times that gnawed holes in my insides.
I wonder now if that is how the very old feel
when they say they want to die.
The novelist wrote, "You can't go home again".
Still, what I want and cannot have,
what so many old and dying seem to crave,
is essence of old home, and being there.

Woman And Kitten

My attention riveted to the photo my husband has taken,
starkly close–up, I ask silently, in all innocence,
"Who is that old woman, with the thin white wiry hair?
the sun–damaged skin,
with the red blotches on neck and chin?
Who's the old lady with the red eyes?
Who's holding my kitten
with her gnarly, deformed fingers?
Whose fat neck and arms are those?

I only allow myself views in one mirror for many years now.
The medicine cabinet mirror over the sink
is two feet away from me. And kind.
I walk past the shop windows facing away, even when I've
no companion to look at, not wanting to own the vision
of that limping, unspirited bulk of face and body.
My daughter, young and fresh of hair and eye,
places her cheek near mine and forces us in front
of the mirror, but I keep my focus on her.

I do not feel that old, that wrinkled, that fat,
that unfit, that washed out, that gone.
So, for a while, I'll not acknowledge with my eyes
the sight of the imposter.

But One Backward Glance

I envy memories
of dreams, of childhood
(mine are limited
to one, or less, a year)

I envy memories
of time before now
of former convictions
(didn't I always believe thus?
this seems so right)

I envy memories
of relationships before
they became memories
of times just before
I rested my head on a shoulder
or clasped a hand

I envy memories
of what I was told as a child
of who told it and how
Did I grow up from that
or down into non–memory?

But envy takes its toll
Perhaps more than all those
memories would. I'll have to
give it up, get on with my now.

Humility

the upturned faces
of children give me pause
whatever else we have done
to ruin our world
however else we have spoiled
the very nature of our ecology
we have yet to change or mar
the upturned grace
of yet one face
of any child looking up to us
to us as though somehow
we are responsible
for this splendor of life

Retiree's Regret

For years I repeated, endlessly,
a million things that didn't need repeating.
A lifelong teaching habit
that I couldn't break even when I realized
the uselessness of rote without example.

Methods, like repeating, gave me means,
I thought, and tools and wherewithal for reaching.
But the unreachables gave not one flicker
of an eye or bate of breath for all my methods.

I learned, finally and late, that if I didn't touch
I didn't teach, regardless of repeating.
I learned to meet the eyes, to clasp the hands.
And now I mourn the ones I didn't touch.

A Thankful Heart

I am grateful for this life,
glad that this particular circle
of knowing and nonconformity
graced my stay.

Perhaps not particularly worthy,
but what's of worth or value
save the dance
within the set we chose
or who chose us?

Children and friends,
wings, flowers, smiles,
air balloons and bicycles,
pictures to ache the eyes,
loves to magnify the heart,
blooms and words that
brought me to my knees —
all gladdened my being
and happied my way,
that was not the way, by far,
that I had thought I'd take.

Connection in Worried Times

Today I am near to bursting with sublime happiness
(in spite of the horrors our rulers embroil us in):
because the forsythia bloomed;
because the rain with sun gleaming through
lit the cocky head of that jay;
because those tulips pushed up through and won;
because the rich soil crumbles in my hands.

If I can still connect here on my knees,
peace and hope are yet and always attainable.
If I can plant broccoli and cabbage in the rain,
watch them grow, then eat what I have grown;
if I can resist man's poisons, I may yet know my place.
If my bread and wine are the grapes I canned
and the loaf I kneaded, I can yet commune.

I Want Poetry and Song

If I go in summer,
throw the windows open
that sun and wind and birdsong
enter in and lift the hearts.
Grateful hearts are
what the world's about.

If I leave in winter,
be happy that the winter hours
are long and rich.
Look upon the frozen world
and stand still and be amazed
at absolute and perfect silence.

If I should die in autumn,
my favorite season,
bask in technicolor splendor.
Watch birds gather up for flight,
then take off in one determined spirit,
seeking perpetuation and reward.

If it's spring that takes me,
know the surety of life too young to see
caught momentarily inside the old, then
unfurling into miracle. Reach out and grab
a moment of that wonder for your own.
Hold it close and keep it with you.

Then sing and play some songs for me.
And read aloud some poems.
Know that I believed that very life —
the now, the then, the yet–to–be —
is poetry and song.

Epilogue with Stars, 2007

I think I saw the flash of you last night —
Not worth, perhaps, the 48 hundred bucks,
Nor the fun of a sparkler,
And I was glad I had fortified me
With a bottle of wine beforehand —
But I do believe I saw you,
A living Dot of quivery light,
Just off the rooftop to the west.

Of course it may have been a speck
Of dust that blew into my eye;
Or it might have been Tim (In Person) Leary,
But I saw something at this time,
Ten years after February, '97,
When ridiculous blended with sublime
To make the weird and final ride
For the twenty–four of you.

Well, many have paid dearer
For a shot at Heaven, and bought less.

On February 11, 1997, Celestis Inc., a company based in Houston, Texas announced that it will next month launch capsules into space containing the cremated remains of 24 people, several of them celebrities in their life. The company is charging $4,800 each for its services. The capsules are expected to orbit the earth up to 10 years before burning up on reentry into the atmosphere.

Post Midnight Encounter

It is the sound that brings me out,
out to the outside dark
I was never one to venture into.
Not a clarion sound, this,
but a summons still,
a call to me, to me personally, I sensed.

Still... but why?

So I could see that thing
the sound had called me about?
See the dome and ring
of darkened windows,
like panel after panel of privacy glass
in a wide dark circle?
See the great overhang
of this thing, pervading
the two houses, the driveway
and every sense that I had?

See that noiseless instant
passing off toward the northwest?
Like an eyeblink, I recall.
That fast! then gone.

I can only wonder still,
many decades later,
what was it I saw?
Why did it call to me?
What unknown lurks, and crawls yet,
just underneath the thin membrane
of my memory's skin?

The Human Condition

Collections

I love the stones that the waves
    have tossed
and tumbled and polished, perfected,
    then lost.
I love to think of what waters
    they've crossed
before ending up here at my feet.

I love the people whom life
    has tossed
and battered and beaten, and given
    for lost.
With suffering and needing their faces
    are crossed,
And their souls are ineffably
    sweet.

Call Out Our Name

We're kindly faces braced before a storm,
bared of all save a mortal, stark concern.
But in the frightening wind we're laughing,
laughing with the seas and skies on rampage,
though we've bitter things to remember.

We're Humankind.

You know the kind we are:
those that Hitler tried to extinguish,
those the Pharaohs kept enslaved,
those the white men on horses stole
gold from, and gave pox to,
those the Klan believed inferior,
those the CIA writes off,
those the "straights" think immoral,
those Nixon tried laughing at,
and later feared and ran from,
those Cheney and Bush think
must be removed from off their path,
those that priests deigned to corrupt,
those whom every New World Order
wants to own and to control.

On a registry somewhere a Wise One
lifts a gilded pen to touch the page.
He smiles at those who have been done to,
and kindly says, "Let it be here recorded
that these, beloved all, are Humankind."

The Conquest

He was a hard, mean man,
as hard as the clods of earth that broke his hoe.
He gave himself no favors,
and expected none from life.
The tiny bit of softness in him
he reserved for his quiet wife.

He had two girls,
daughters of a younger mating;
and though one, the older,
took to the gentle ways of her stepmother,
and grew subdued and soft,
even to her own dependence,
the other resembled him
in harsh and proud defiance.

This one, then, the proud,
he sought to tame.
She hoed along his side,
took clod for clod of rocky ground.
She drove the tractor,
slopped the hogs,
all with mean, dire looks
and angry mutterings.

She smiled at him with narrowed eyes
and mouth of arrogance,
then hid and sneaked away
at every chance.
At church she dared to run
when his eye had turned
from her to heaven;
then she rolled with the boys
in the mossy shade in the graveyard
behind the manse.

No liquor or tobacco
had ever passed his lips;
so she drank home–brew
in the trucks of the wildest boys
and out–smoked them all
in the orchard behind the barn.

Her father preached of the
evil ways of the young,
and she crawled out the window
and climbed down the tree
to meet with the town's worst wastrels.
The old man screamed that
"The wages of sin is death!"
Then she found herself with child.

She sought to kill the life within
with a hanger bent to a hook.
The old man climbed to the loft
to fork down the evening hay,
and found her dead in a pool of blood.

It took six strong men to carry
the old one off, a broken,
slobbering, terror–filled wretch
who swaggled his hands and arms
in aimless jerking circles,
who babbled of the River Jordon,
then curled to a fetal shape
and wept away a half a hundred
years of crust and shell of meanness.

He was fetal–shaped
when they bore him off,
one hand shielding both eyes,
the other over an ear.
Fetal–shaped still when his heart stopped
in less than a day.

Defeat

A little snort from a tiny flask behind the door
before the straightened back and sigh
propel him to the mike, wan smile pasted on.

He's already watched on the tube her thin
tight–lipped grasping of the day, followed
by a brilliant smile, her eyes, though,
remaining two mean knife slashes.

He must concede. His friends are waiting.
Concede to someone tougher than himself.
His Daddy had warned that politics
was for the tough. And tough she was.
On crime, on immigrants (you'd think
to hear her talk, that her folks hadn't
even come from somewhere), on unions,
on small farmers, and small hopes.

He'd bet she could face anyone and anything
and stare them down, then smile at them,
without one snort, one snort to fortify her.

Master Gardener

She'd done it all by the book:
covered, staked and fertilized,
even companion–planted,
to Joe's great glee,
those damned garlic bulbs.
She bought lady bugs for aphids,
trimmed dead stems, composted,
soap sprayed, pinched back buds,
carried out all the endless gardener's rites.

She collected sweet bouquets that season,
then another, and still another of perfection.
To go with the cuttings she collected
she gathered up precious compliments.
Joe compared her smooth blushed cheek
to her armload of tea roses.
Her garden club awarded her that fall
with its coveted Rose Plaque.
Then came the hard winter of '96:

The frost went deep, rock hard.
The wind chill plummeted, while
cold's tenacious grip froze, uprooted,
cracked ground near tender roots.
Then it froze again, briefly thawed,
then did it all once more.
In May there were no green leaves budding.
If you scraped the thick stalks,
you met only with dry dust and pith.

Her marriage hadn't wintered either,
so she shed no tears for roses.

No Public Display Of

On our trip to the botanical gardens
we observed nearly all the amenities:
stayed off the grass
only walked on pebbled paths,
didn't imitate that statuary
of nude dancers.

Midnight didn't find us
clasped together by that flashing fountain
where, after carefully looking both ways,
we'd kissed so briefly.
(One small error perhaps,
un tres petit faux pas,
not magnified, not repeated.)
Propriety's alive and well
in this north Texas city.

They may read in the Sunday rag
that blue–haired teens get arrested
for romping in the buff
around those wild steeds
in the waters at Las Colinas;
but we two, in notable decorum,
walk side by side without touching
to the theatre matinee,
and sit, sharing nothing but
our laughter and a popcorn bucket.

Are we a little weird to save it all
for us and unobserved?
Would they ever believe it is
our own selfishness instead
of the teachings of Miss Manners?

Forging

When she got very homesick,
she made cheese,
pressed under a brick on the windowsill
of her tiny kitchen.

She thought of Mama
and of the futility of
trying hard to call.

Though she did call frequently,
screaming "Mama!" from
out of her dark lost dreams.

Those times she'd thump her brain
against the reality of death
and sob until the blessed escape
into sleep again,
a sleep sometimes delayed
until drugged.

Mothers and daughters, she thought,
need strong, indissoluble chains
to connect. Don't outgrow the need.
May not even survive without it,
and death can't dismiss it.

On some mornings after
she'd salt and eat the cheese,
spread on a bagel,
and nibbled very slowly.
Not as good as Mama's, she'd think.
Not a chain at all, in fact,
but, just perhaps, a link.

The Dreamers

In sleep we turn
And, turning, our foreheads touch:
Your dreams and mine cross over,
    Yours blending quickly with my own
    Mine melding softly into yours.
The dream–bond tying us two
As tightly as did the wedding band,
But mystically newer, irretrievable.

In the morning
We cannot speak of it. Beyond awe,
It crowds our day, and pushes out the boundaries
    Of what we knew of rational
    Of what we could think possible.
Only at the dusk can we confess it,
Staring ahead, not facing ridicule, then
Weeping, turn and let our foreheads kiss.

Family Photo Album

We are frozen into photographs in time,
yellowed, faded, cracked, with edges torn.
We look out now from a past we scarce remember,
locked there, caught with such a stare or smile
we can't define or understand in any way
except, sometimes, a mute and dull acceptance
that it, indeed, was us on that particular day.

Yet, when memories of us do assail us,
it is not of this or that posed or candid picture,
but of us essential, the raw and feeling us
that hurts or laughs, or loves or hates anew
with every memory scrap that beats upon our minds.
Then those aging photos, purported to be worth
a thousand words, are no good to us at all.

Out of the Mist

It was a foggy morning.
Fogged inside and out,
he tried to shake himself awake
without the sun.

As he left for work
only the first ten feet were clear.
Suddenly those limits closed upon
his very future, his whole life.

He felt an ancient cry
rise up from deep for God's help.
He'd not been a praying man,
but this was different, an appetite

that rose from some primeval part
of him he didn't know existed.
He almost shouted, "God!", but
caught himself up in alarm

feeling out of control, and lost.
The outline of the city was so dim
it was no longer his. He needed... what?
an hour alone? some time to sort?

He turned and headed home. He'd not
be missed one day. A glad anxiety shook him.
He could barely wait to fall upon his knees
and duke it out with God.

The Theft

Jerry, you have copped this day from me,
have stolen it and run.
My mom's purse–snatcher warnings,
her tales of crime upon the streets,
never told me that on a quiet beach
in day's full sun someone I trusted
perfectly could so deceive, and rob, and run.

It was one of those days, so super special,
on a calendar of rare ones, I'd been thanking it since dawn.
You took it, all the rest of it, away, and left me here
deprived and weeping 'cause it's gone. Jerry!
Just how could you take my day?

Jerry, you might have left me something
of it, taste, perhaps, or smell,
or just the hint of sunset on the sea.
You could have left a single second of it to me.
But no, you had to take it all: to spend, or live,
or throw down in disgust,
or just to take it 'cause it's mine
so you felt somehow you must.
Jerry, how did you have the crust?

I'll get it back, you know.
I'll turn you in, fill out a full report.
For I have its description and your name.
And you'll know that, when they come for you,
it's more than just a game of Take and Seek.
I'll get my day back if it takes me all next week!

Jerry, could you maybe bring it back tomorrow?
We could work out something, I am sure.
And I'll not press charges if you show the proper sorrow
and remorse, and pay me a little interest on it
later on this year. Perhaps I'll even let you
smooth talk me into giving you a share.
Why! It's you, Jerry, back here with my day!
Tell me, how long have you been standing there?

The Keepers

She played with them,
the many cats,
the several husbands.
Took them in,
cleaned them up,
fed them,
and caressed them.

Then, if things didn't work out,
like: they didn't clean their feet,
had messy eating habits,
or sang on occasion
utterly fiendish songs,
they'd have to make it on their own.
She opened her door and pointed: Out.

I, however,
having found one of each
that needed a home, thought:
they'll just have to put up with my bad habits.

Post Script:

She sits alone now in her perfect house,
figurines and plants intact,
no claw marks on her sofa,
and no contented purring at her feet
or ardent kisses on her neck.

The Job

The young woman,
wings pinned on,
bends over the passenger.

It was for excitement
she has not found
that she sought the job.

From taxi to hotel to airport
to fresh old men
or young ones calling her.

Usually in a rush,
with nothing but sleep to snatch
at the other end.

Smells of smoke or perfume
or worse, much worse, assail her.
Now and then small and
unpleasant emergencies.

Several days in a lump
in some large city she doesn't know,
except its distance from home,
then rush again, taxi to airport.

"Marry me!" the man with bold eyes
bursts out again, as she turns her back,
and once more smiles, "Coffee or tea?"

Irreconcilable Differences

His pale feet were smooth as baby–skin,
hers scratchy from a summer's garden clods
as they sat bare upon the river bank,
feet dangling off the edge.
She felt ashamed of her brown and sturdy limbs,
compared them to the whiteness of his legs and feet,
feet like you'd turned a rock and found grass
gone all white from lack of sun.

"The roots of Mother Earth grow into me,"
she said. "I feel them throbbing under, through me.
And when you men march, feet encased
in boots of leather, toes of steel,
you can't even know it when our tendril's cut.
And we're left bleeding here, and severed.

"Then a part of me, my arms, must reach up
and grow into the trunks and branches
of my Mother's trees. And when you men,
in spiked boots for puncturing,
climb this trunk and cut, your chainsaws
slice through my Mother's ancient calm,
wake her from sleeping. The whining noise,
the fumes, the grit of flying sawdust
make us wince and writhe in pain."

"We must not kill Her," she cried out,
"or we too will die. Her warning's in an ancient
tongue, feels torn from my aching throat!"

"Oh, you women gripe my ass!" he swore.
"You want it all —
your microwaves,
your plushy cars,
your fancy furniture and clothes.
But listen up:
the piper must be paid.
Your precious mother's got to be the cost
of all the unnatural stuff you keep demanding!"

Then he angrily dressed, pulled on his shorts,
covered the white smooth feet with socks,
put on his boots, brushed off his trouser legs,
shrugged himself into his discarded shirt, and left her,
small and curled and brown,
a lump of hurting, part of very earth.

Usada

In the window of a used–clothing store
    Ropa usada
In the window once–worn finery I've never seen before
    Usada
Then I stare transfixed at the wedding gown she wore
    O usada! Usada!

The studded tiara that had graced her sleek black hair
    Usada Usada
That pouf–sleeved bodice she'd arranged with such a care
    O Usada
Yards of lacy skirt that no one else should ever wear
    My heart broken and Usada

Who she went with that night she felt no need to confess
    Usada Usada
But to pay for flight she sold the rings and sold the dress
    O Usada
If she could, she'd have sold my stolen happiness
    And I'm left alone here, and Usada

To the Innocents

He is a waiter.
Not patient, though,
but, rather, coiled steel,
each nerve a taut–stretched bow.
Eyes eagle–sharp,
waiting for a tiny weakness
to become apparent,
then attack!
He is a waiter.

Waiters voice sounds of abasement:
May–I–help–you, want–to–serve–you
kinds of things. His subservience
masks his base motives.

As a sleek cat waits in the grasses;
while the huge hawk waits on the wires;
and the poised egret waits knee–deep in mud,
so the drug dealer waits in the shadows.
They bide time. They watch. And they wait.
He is a waiter.

Pain

The child swung and swung in the willow tree swing,
headphones on, eyes closed, hair blowing out behind.
Her prescription for the hollowness and pain for which
she had no name in those years leading up to
and during the divorce was to go each day to the swing.
With her tapes and her songs she could calm out
the raging storms of their quarrels and find haven.

Her older brother's solution was all self–torment.
He went only as far as the porch steps
where he could still hear their words.
Hearing, he would whittle viciously,
or beat his baseball bat against the steps
or kick one foot against the other, forcing different pain.
He heard the voices he had loved turn into hate.

Later, the girl–turned–woman was to treat each parent
with the long love of collected respect and maturity.
She brought them home to care for when they ailed.
She arranged memorials of love and calmness when they died.

The man–who'd–been–boy couldn't trust himself not to despise,
feared commitments, marriage, siring children,
was brisk, sometimes brutal, with women he knew,
became a cold, unsympathetic employer.
He would not attend the services for his parents, his betrayers.

One More Indignity at the Nursing Home

She sits with a frown and vacant eyes,
and hands that rise and fall again
as if to protest all of this if she were able.
She cannot dress herself, or lift a spoon,
or say one word to tell us why of anything.

She cut her own toenails before,
this quiet, private woman,
wouldn't even have her hair done
save by a trusted daughter;
yet here the snip and crunch is done
by under–paid caregivers.
We may be all the name implies,
but not in this old lady's eyes.
She's not relaxed, just bearing.

Strange how those words "bear up"
took on almost a glory once,
as widows and orphans and the otherwise
bereft were told it would be wrong
to show or share a grief that had blown
or pounded their lives to pulverized
particulates. Strange anyone should
ever think stored passion better.

I wish that she would scream at me,
or slap my hand away, or curse,
for nothing could be worse
than the cross this lady's wearing.

Summer Job–Hunt

The thought of caring for hundreds of hummingbirds
(numerous species of which the great
Sonoran desert was renowned)
had charmed her.

The ad and phone call
held forth romance enough
to fill her head with mystery and excitement.

She thought of Jane Eyre,
captivating conversations
with bright people over tea,
all the elegant excitement
of an Angela Lansbury escapade.

She pictured them
on a shaded, screened–in porch,
cool drinks in hand,
she being finally persuaded
by the lady's guests to play for them
a little Brahms or Debussy after dinner.

She would assist the elder gentlewoman
to identify the various species,
watch her employer lift gem–encrusted binoculars
to aged eyes and admit, with a most gracious smile,
that her new companion had indeed corrected her mistake.

It started well:
a maid to cook and clean,
and herself to be paid room and board
and a small stipend for important other "duties".

But the first day set the tone:
How could she have known the lady
had actually cared for the birds herself?
"Female companion to elderly bird–lover,
must love and want to care for many birds,"
the ad had stated, but she hadn't dreamed that
she would be expected to clean and fill
every feeder, every day, up and down hill!

Her own arthritis, her own fastidiousness rebelled.
She mumbled her apologies and fled.
Her visions shattered, she uttered unladylike obscenities
on the long, hot drive back to town.
She couldn't believe "companion" could include
Birdshit!

Bed Scene, 4 A. M.

He snored his crazy snores,
the silly ones with laugh attached
to each, the ones that used to drive
her from the bed, or make her laugh,
or screech his name till he came
groggily up from sleep,
confused, apologetic.

Now she simply gathered up
the sheets about herself and smiled
and kept fond vigil. For he'd been gone
for too long, and for far too far,
for such a dead time out–of–reach,
that her hand of its volition clasped
his bare shoulder, crying, "Stay!"

She thought of her long
hibernation while he was away —
no sun, no parties, and no dancing,
no laughing till she cried. For joy
had crawled up somewhere deep
inside, and, malnourished, starving, died.

Strange, though, how all those years
that he'd been gone, in all that time,
he'd never left her side.

Judgment

How he yearned for a good wife,
To cook and to sew and to mend.
I can't mend much but a child's bruised knee,
Or a ruined wet Sunday,
Or your tired sore back with my kisses.
Will I do? Will I do?

How he longed for a good wife,
To do sums, to clean house, to make do.
My sums are: a bushel of peaches canned,
A dozen pies, ten bouquets,
Three small faces smiling at six stories read,
And a poem I wrote just for you.
Will I do?

How he would adore a good wife,
Ironing done, floors fresh–waxed, meals on time.
I only can bring you some sun–warmed sheets,
Midnight meals of apples and cheese,
And a kitchen floor bright with the tumbling of kids
Chasing kittens around, on their knees.
Will I do?

Parting

His last words hung in the air
like a summation speech,
though lawyers tend more to plea
than to issue ultimatums.

You will — I will — this means —
I'm going — I'll make — I want —
Hey, wait! Hang on a minute!
Where's it written the accused can't bat an eye?

Miranda doesn't witness my tears,
copious as water from the dog's bath.
I scream my accusations too,
though no officer of law has said a word.

How does sharing drift across a span
that turns it into ownership?
When did we say or not say, do or not do,
those things that locked it in?

Hard to think now, how it was then,
the delicacy, the graceful nuance,
the earnest desire to try to understand;
but I felt it die now in one small beat of time.

I'd like to wash it off of me,
the words of the last ten minutes,
but I know it's more indelible
than the stains of the contract ink.

The Human Condition

One Day of Life

Small change for a dish of pork and beans.
It's not my style to order steak.
After full hour following full hour
of house and kids, radios and clocks
bringing incessant insanity of time
to my already chaos, what do I need of time?

I marvel that the lazy cat,
life and limb in unknowing danger,
stretches one long black leg and then
the other straight out behind.
(but I'm not that free, or bored.)

Spring has to follow March;
it's just the wishing that it would
that kills. A little inside storm
pushes from the boundaries of my brain,
as I watch, detached, my suds billowing
overflow at the laundromat.

Now the bus returns with them
(it couldn't take it either.),
and spits forth kids. Running feet,
barking dogs, hugs, jostles, tumbling
on the rug. Papers, books go flying
with excited recountings of the day.
Screams and tears and "What's to eat?"
Excited tuggings at my hands.
All this at ear–split level, traumatizing
my shy former solitude into full retreat.
Viva! You win! Time called! Uncle! I give!
Enough reward already!

Quarrel II

I know
it looks like I've accomplished
nothing in your absence,
but I've thought, and prayed a lot.
Such things take time.

And I've worked
to put me in the proper
state of mind for your return.
Decided how my greeting
must be spoken, lest
that slender thread that
joined us even as you walked
be now, for all time, broken.

I've verified,
and tidied up, and neatly packaged
all those things I didn't, couldn't
say, and put them all away.

No, not put them to the flame!
For doesn't blame, like rain,
fall down upon us all in season?
The reason that I've saved them
is that one day I may find a need
for all I've kept, if nothing more
than for remembrance
when you have left.

I realize
there're papers, books alitter
on the table. Yes,
I recognize them. They're my work.
And when I'm able I will sort
and clear, and make a space,
and set your place for food. So
don't be rude and start again.
For you have work outside; it's your domain.
That's fine. Let me have mine.

No, I didn't pay for the insurance,
cash those checks, or spray the roses.
I haven't that endurance when my
heart is hurting. There is no reposing
when you leave, not when all that's left
to me, or so it seems, is just to grieve.

Well, here we go once more.
It's just no use. The two of us
seem only capable to look for,
and to find, but one excuse,
just one, to set us off.
But before you slam that door
and go off somewhere again.
I offer a suggestion. No, not that
in fact. It's just a question, only
one: just what did *you* get done
while you were gone?

Pioneers Unsieged

She cooked a huge pot of butter beans, to celebrate
we were eating anything at all,
and parched some old corn,
dusty from hanging from the attic rafters.

She didn't say anything, just nodded us to the table.
It was quiet while we ate and ate, all of us and her.
Then, "It's late," her voice a tired bludgeon to the silence.
"Go fetch the cow and milk her.
Mind, catch the gate now,
can't afford to lose that critter."

I walked in wary, muddy steps, feeling watched.
But at least the corn and beans had stuffed my belly.
And suddenly I felt sure, brightening,
that she'd let us have warm milk tonight
before our bed because we were alive.
Life does little self–congratulatory dances
on its own after it's been threatened.

They hadn't won this night,
hadn't given us the shellacking we'd all feared,
hadn't beaten us up or raped us,
hadn't put us off this farm we'd found and built on.

"God–damned Squatters," they'd shouted, riding up.
One ugly voice rang out when they saw us
with all the little ones peeking from around Ma's skirts,
"Hell! It's just a woman and a bunch of kids.
Let's go! She sure can't do us no harm!"
He hawkered up and spat toward Ma who stood
holding the mob to inaction with her unflinching shotgun.

Finally, their eyes had lost the battle
with Ma's tough and narrowed brown ones,
and they'd turned, mumbling, guiding their way
back to town with the torches they'd brought
and hoped to burn us out with.

For most of a year after, Ma and I kept
the little ones close by us as we worked.
For most of that year I walked with swiveling neck,
afraid I'd see those ugly flames again.
For months I'd hear those coarse voices
and see those mean eyes searching for scapegoats,
probably jealous that some could make a home
while all they could make was trouble.

Ebenezer

Ebenezer was a farmer down the rutted lane.
Aggie was his wife, a good and tidy soul.
The boy and his mother rented a tiny house
from them nearby. Ebenezer was his mentor.
His mother and Aggie judged how Ebenezer
ought to go to church or, at the very least, Revival.
    But Ebenezer wouldn't.

When the August sun burned down too hot
to work the fields afternoons, Ebenezer napped
on top of old Hemmingway Gazettes spread
out all along the couch, while Aggie fumed
with hands on hips, "You'll be the death of me!
At least take off them mud–caked shoes!"
    But Ebenezer didn't.

Some Sundays the boy and the grizzled old man
would sit for hours on wooden apple crates
at the edge of the water where an ambling stream
curved back and out across the farm.
And the boy would close his eyes and pray
his oft–repeated prayer, "Wish he could be my dad."
    But Ebenezer couldn't.

At the county fair the old man felt young again
and challenged all the others in a mule–pull.
He slipped in the mud and fell with a grab at the reins,
while the startled mule lashed out with his hooves behind.
Aggie wrung her hands and flustered round and wailed,
"You poor old fool! You'd oughta had some sense!"
    But Ebenezer hadn't.

They cleaned off the mud. The doctor shook his head.
They put him in a coffin on a satin pillow.
The boy stood and wondered if they'd left his muddy shoes on,
if there was, maybe, old newspapers underneath him.
If Aggie had said it once, she'd said it a thousand times,
"Ebenezer, you'll be the death of me!"
    But Ebenezer wasn't.

Highway Tragedy

"You see," she said, "it tore the heart from me.
We'd just come from the church;
there was this sudden lurch.
My life was torn, me a wife of just one morn.
He sat by me (we each the other's world)
as through a deafening space we hurled.
They tell me he was killed instantly.
It's lies they give, for they tell me I will live.
They tell me that it's he who died instead,
as, inch–by–inch, I die upon this bed."

"A very strange case," the doctor said.
"As you can see, all her wounds are healed.
(Her young husband, as you know, is dead.)
She seems to hold a psychic shield
against her healing. Her bones have knit,
but her pulse grows weaker bit by bit.
The gashes are but pink and puckered lines,
but each breath's so weak it can hardly be defined.
Her mind's not even here. Her emotionless face
shows no sign of knowing or of pain or fear."

Legacy

He pinched them
(for luck? for reality check?),
pinched each and every cent
that went into his coffers.
I don't say he loved them all.
Does a man love every rounded bottom
that he pinches in a dusky bar?
But how he squeezed and rubbed them.

And he counted.
Perhaps it was the counting act he loved the most.
But he certainly loved the totals,
for he read them out as proud
as if he had invented adding.

Seeing those totals in print,
in the monthly or quarterly statements,
or written in his slow laborious hand
at the bottom of each column,
was the very apex of his joy.

Small wonder, then,
having pinched and added,
totaled up and printed out, and loved the sum,
small wonder he was loath to shrink it down
by any least amount.

Oh, he spent a little.
Man has to eat and heat his home
and cover up his nudity some way.
And he bought minute insurances
by wrestling out a few small bills
when the plate was passed
(just in case there might be truth
about the needle's eye, and all).
But it was with pain
that he subtracted any coin
that he'd caressed, a scratchy, achy
soreness when he'd done,
kind of how the throat feels
after vomiting, it was.

He felt his loss.
He could barely wait until
the very next check or bit of cash appeared
to tidy up that empty hole
left by his spending.

Each January first, as a New Year's gift,
he read aloud, to his well–provided–for,
but hungry and needy, family his year's net worth.
Read the figures forth in a voice
so clear and steady and loud
it had to be the one thing he was proudest of.
They listened, were properly impressed,
then breathed again and went their ways to fill,
as inexpensively as possible, their days.

Each family member believed
that he or she was poor.
Each scrimped and went without.
None had knowledge or belief
that any difference could exist.
The New Year's Numbers stood
on high before them, like Mount Rushmore,
to acknowledge, not to touch.
They never criticized, or even seemed
to notice much, his miser's ways,
accepted what was, with a quiet bearing, almost cheer.

Yet when he died, that family blew
away his meager fortune in the year.

Road Widow

Sleepless
She watches the highway lights
Through fog–grayed window
Slow tonight
blip....blip....blip
enter....cross....disappear
blip....blip....blip
like a heart monitor
Sometimes she nearly panics
As it flat–lines

Her county's all vast, flat farmland
The highway he's on, a straight line
That crosses her window as she waits
Alone in her bed without him
Headlights come fitfully now, and scarce
blip..........blip..blip.......blip

Carefully
She's learned to live right on the edge
When he leaves, and his semi blips
Across some other windows, other states
blip........blip........blip
And she's sharp–honed, now, her intuition
Intuition she must live by
Intuition flushed with hope for his safe return

On the Sanctity of Beans
for Juanita's Mom

No one had told her she must put aside
her grief and, somehow, feed a crowd.
She and Jake had stayed apart
and left to others all those social rules.
Busy filled their hours with simply making–do.

But she was game. Long illness of a loved one,
tending, caring, leaves you anything but gameless.
She just hadn't known that Jake had known
so many people, that they'd had so many friends.

She hurried to her cupboard then to see
if she had means, something filling and substantial.
She couldn't send them hungry on their way.
"Where are those loaves and fishes, Damn it!"
she cried out. (She'd sworn a lot at God
these last few months, as Jake's health eroded,
stumbled, faltered, died and finally gone.)

Canned beans. A cupboard full, put by
this summer past, between her nursing
and her cursing. She didn't ask if beans were fit to serve,
only prayed that there would be enough.

And as that whole long afternoon wore on —
with person after person, some she'd hardly met,
filing past the rough–hewn coffin —
she'd opened up yet another jar of beans
and baked more cornbread. It was enough.

Curiously, she found her shelves quite full of beans
when all had eaten and gone home.

Odors of Aging

Her menses petered out for six months,
then left altogether in a cold January.
Good. She was relieved.
Her fastidious nose was relieved.
She could do with a rest anyway.

Nearly gone, too, was the smell of fertility
as it dwindled, then disappeared.
It's absence left her with nostalgia,
with a gentle case of self–pity.
To be androgynous, literally "unattractive",
worse than the thinning hair,
worse than the soft paper skin tissues
crinkling, rearranging her face
was her womanness saying its finality.

But now, also, her nose was glad.
If she'd be sent to sit on the iceberg,
what devouring thing could tell?
Would the lack stay the polar bear?

She'd been modern woman, fighting
to rid herself of what must once have been
the beacon that kept the race renewed.
The odor that worried her, and that
commercials warned her of for most of her life,
the under–arm result of exertion —
it itself, perhaps, past flame to ancient man
when manual work was needed,
and its aftersmell spelled survival —
one day was only a memory.

She left off buying deodorant
and liked this coasting time, feeling cleansed.

Then, so light at first as to be almost not there,
a smell replaced the other three, a sourness.
A sour aroma drifting up from all of her
with no special places to apply deodorant
or to wear perfume, just sourness, like a sickness
over–all, assaulting her nostrils.

She stepped from the bath to smell
it again within minutes, showered to have it
return nearly at once, scrubbed furiously
but couldn't rid herself more than
momentarily, watched people's faces
to see if she was offensive.

This the commercials avoided;
this was not taught in health class;
this was not passed on to daughters.
For who would ever believe?
Who could know that the final odor
could not be washed away?
Who even knew about the sour smell
of age, of rank decay, of death?

She prayed fervently that all smells
would end with this one, that this
unwashable not proceed to an
irrevocable return to the infant–oblivious
        smell of urine.

Final Word

I've had to withdraw from your
recriminations
accusations
insinuations
assumptions
allegations
suppositions
noninclusions,
I was left with no choice.

I used to think, and say, that
we fought with what
weapons we had, but I've
found that I have none.
A pacifist's only 'weapon'
is retreat, and so I go.
We began on uneven ground,
though I didn't know it then.

In Praise Of Nature

I Would Have Cosmos

The peace of the flowers,
delicate, fragile, sunset–hued,
bending first to right,
and then to left in peaceful swaying.

My Mother sketched them
once with pencil–crayons.
How I marveled at my mother the artist,
noticed for the first time the jagged petals,
saw pollen dusting on shiny tabletop.
My Mother Earth the Artist
drew them in the original.

I've always loved the cosmos
since I first learned their name,
white and rose and purple,
swaying colors at the end of day.
Now I find them vibrant yellow and orange!
Peace not dying but aborning.

Forest and Tree

We stood up high along the ridge
to view without telescope,
to experience that vastness of distance
    across
        and out
           and beyond.

But I found myself —
    as the teasing sunlight
    in slanted glare
    progressed down the mountain,
    in and out of clouds,
    and made arrow shafts of brilliance
    glancing off those mineraled
    mirrors in my view —
longing for a magnifying glass
to better see the whiff of blue flower leaf,
clinging, with no apparent means, to the rock
situated just there,
beyond my toe.

Old Adages Die Hard
And So Do Violets

For sheer pushiness and power
I'll choose the violet every time,
tenacious as a clam.

In spring before the mowers start
it crowds out both grass and weeds
and lays a purple carpet at our feet.

It produces offspring myriad
which spread throughout my rock garden,
pushing, shading, dwarfing,
clamoring for room,
forcing my store–bought flowers
to cower and yellow and forget to grow.

Violets just can't be shy,
and certainly not shrinking.
Now who first thought that lie?

Du Bois

Lily of the Valley,
attar and essence of God,
that May should come
and not bring your delight
were hurt untenable.

Tiny bells that graced
my mother's grave
and lit the shoulder of my
bridal dress, you calm me now
with faith unshakable.

May it is, and another
May I have attained
by your wee proof of it.
Fear that spring would not be mine,
this now joy not be gained
is now unthinkable.

Sun Seeds

Seeds of sun they are
and food fit for angels,
evocative of lordship.

In the garden
their great lion heads
turn in one day
against all odds
    to face their mother
    to keep pace with their strength
    to acknowledge their beginning
    to bow to their source.

Finally, on the day
when those great stalks of necks
can do no more
than droop in shame,
the cardinals come to steal,
and the squawking jays,
scolding others off, to feed.

Then the fast–food bars
serve them up,
with no hint of their mystery,
of the power nutrition sealed within,
or of their recent history.

Reciprocity

We have a sparrow bush that plays,
in springs and summers, at being
merely ornamental spirea.

Then, when snow comes to lay
its spotless spread across the ground
and drape with glistening garlands

all the trees, the little brown jobbies
elect this one bush to festoon
with their own mottled, rounded bodies.

Close by the feeder and close against the house
this one bush holds a score or two
between their flits to feed and peck out

the grit that's part of our home's foundation.
The house will not soon miss the small
particulates of the birds' digestion,

for it has stood more than a century now
without showing too much stress caused
by this passive generous sharing of

those minute amounts of the largess
of its very structure to sustain those visitors
who now give heart to wintered eyes.

Late July Rendezvous

Come meet me by the forest edge
at blackberry–picking time.
Our tryst will be a feast.
But only if you've daring
and the grace of fortitude and pluck;

for it's not that miniscule
and path–o're–hanging fruit
that ends our hungry search,
but the opulence!
The under–and–behind–
and–hidden–in–the–midst–of thorn:
this is the quest.

Shadowed there, and hanging low
in great grape–clumps our prize:
that juicy, oozing royal purple
finger–staining, sweet–tart nectar,
that guarded–by–the–briar treasure.

Then you and I will eat
and fill ourselves content.
We'll lick our wounds,
and carry home our scars,
and know the taste is worth the venture.

The Tourist

Vancouver's rain and I
trot in slippery mud down the steep hill
to look up to the lighthouse.

Obligatory pictures snapped,
I turn and trudge back up a slope
that grows in steepness with my climb.

I hear a bird. Woodpecker?
I wander off the path toward his sound.
What's the hurry?
I can't be wetter.
The bird has attached himself
low on a trunk,
stops and cocks his head at my approach,
but doesn't panic.
I sit suddenly down in a bed of trillium.

The bird quiet, the rain stopped,
the tourists out–of–sight.
It's as though I've never before heard silence,
as though I've never before been alone.
What a piece of timelessness I capture!
I think. I breathe. I wonder.
I spend the longest moments
since the time when I was ten
and hadn't yet met hurry.

Riding back on the bus, I'm all smug.
All these other poor passengers
can't know that bird, those trillium, or that silence.

The Big and the Small of It

Space bores me:
The time
The cost
The concept
And the waste
The brash and boring bigness of the place.

I ho–hummed me
All the way
Through Star Trek
And Star Wars
The stepping on the moon
The moon rock collection
And that chore, stretching life's ecology,
Of pushing all that
Literal gas for launching
Up from all that hot air
Of politicking and financing.

An eleventh century me,
I don't know as I'd join the Fathers
In those discourses about angels
Dancing on the heads of pins,
But the world–in–a–drop–of–water
Concept grabs my respect.

I find more to marvel at
In Poppy seeds than space.
Those concentrated crunchings
In the cake I bake
Or those aromas when I carefully
Sprinkle them on rolls to make
A crusty browned perfection.

I bet myself
That I can't eat just one,
But before I crush it in my teeth
(Grateful for the seeds we've all been given
Out of which to form our roots)
I think about that tiny embryo
And how it's folded snug away
Inside one poppy seed.

Arkansas Winter

All sharp lines and jutting angles,
dead armadillos
Lombardy poplars
and Spanish daggers.

Arkansas folks, dirt poor,
selling the dirt out from under their feet.
Chiseling away at the mountainside.
Peddling their crystals for cures.

Clear and sharp–pointed crystals,
Vying for points with
Spanish daggers,
Lombardy poplars,
and dead armadillos.

12 September, '96

Cool aftermorn of mid–September rain
sends me to the garden for the reunion
that parched August had postponed too long.
I lift the beaten tendrils of late–planted peas
to help them grasp their trellis and hold on.

I check the late beans I had feared for
and find tiny miracles of softest pinkish blooms
(perhaps just overnight, once rain's manna
has poured down). If I had a child now
in this wonderment I feel, I'd name it
Bean Blossom, so that all its life it would stay
reminded of this late season's marvel.

To plant in a sere August is act of foolishness, or Faith.
To find my faith replete, the Perfect Day.

May Ritual

The rocky ground, unyielding,
will not take my spade.
While I, equally stubborn,
claim out loud, "You will!"

We've fought this selfsame battle
every spring from then to now:
it takes quite willingly my seed,
but it will not stand my till.

If I pretend I'm angry,
pretend the soil has won the day,
that last year's plantings
it's allowed to gain strong root
have somehow, in my anger,
missed my eye, it seems content
enough to let me pry a rock
or two away, and smile with
a sweet perennial's frail bloom.

Each spring that I made garden
we've reenacted this charade.
It blossoms with my care, but resists,
against all odds, the forcing of my spade.

The Willow Yellows Twice

In early spring, when not much else
    is hopeful,
pollen drips down along her arms
    to eye's delight.

In fall, after most have dropped their
    dry brown leaves
in giving up, or in disgust, she drapes herself
    again in gold.

When I puzzle if fast–approaching years
    will put their periods
on everything too soon, leaving me not one
    good day more
to joy in, I think about that buttery tree,
    inspiring me,
trailing long and lemony hands into the river,
    and remember that
the willow yellows twice.

Love-in-the-Mist

When I first wake
to nigella by the door,

the day's put on its freshest dress.
I take the time to pause
and really see its sweet
and delicious downy fern.
The whole day's better for it.

In breaths of pale blue to misty white
it pleases 'til the blooming's done,
then charms in brown and crusty pods
which I take inside to admire
for all long winter's non–bloom days

to help me wait
for nigella by the door.

Death And Dying

Where We Go

How do we dare to call a death untimely
when all deaths are.
Even if, in our evaluation,
some death is welcome, the out–of–pain–now kind,
it's only from our viewpoint.

We cannot live inside another's dream
to know if it is fractured beyond mending,
or if its silence is the very apex of its dreaming.
Perhaps when we say sadly that
he doesn't even know me, he's actually found
that better part of knowing. In eclectic wisdom
he may have flown the years to find a peace
that indeed has dimmed all other places
where he has dipped his mind before.
Shutting you out may be the only way
he can place you in the bigger picture.

Dead and Alive

I'd thought our living done.
Finished, the bivouac at the bed.
I ate fully of the bitter herb of grief.

Then, as I solemnly spread
your ashes out
to honor your request,

a sudden gust arose.
You slipped into my eye.
I find I view the world, now,

more as you would. And I've a part
of you to love still, openly,
and to carry with me 'til I die.

April Grief

The sun was slowly warming all creation.
They told me that the birds began to sing.
A crocus boasted color on the snowline.
But I didn't even notice it was spring.

The peepers' voices called out from the swampland.
A butterfly fanned fast his sodden wing.
Small children rushed in, smelling of the freshness.
But I didn't even notice it was spring.

Revival green with hope the lawn was painted.
The daffodil, a splendid golden thing!
I thought that wonder's death had overcome me
For I didn't even notice it was spring.

Sweaters, gloves and hats were all discarded.
And your hands sought me violets to bring.
But me, I kept my winter heart and face on,
For I didn't even notice it was spring.

A Good Day To Die

To burn a certain candle:
Life
or Age
or Love
or simply Growing,
We must have the knowing:
when to snuff it out
when to keep the wick trimmed
when to call a halt
or when the tallow's spent.

When the Moment,
lent to us through ages,
turned through all the pages,
sifted all the sands of all the times,
then names this one sublime
for our leave–taking,
even if not of our own making,

Comes that time, the bargain
that we fashioned, before we
signed our contract, long long ago,
too long for memory–keeping.

That time's, then, not for weeping,
but for grabbing. Grasp the hand
of this new venture!
Indentured to this light no longer
but to something stronger,
bigger, firmer, brighter,
more beatific, lighter,
the time for our Rebirth!

I Mourned That Child

I mourned that child till all the suns went down,
then till they rose again up strong.
Too much of death and dying for this clown.
Too much of pain, injustices, and wrong.

I couldn't understand at all, at all
a tiny rosebud destined not to grow.
And how could she, weeping, stand so very tall,
then say good–by (with thoughts I couldn't know)?

She chose an unmarked grave for resting place.
I covered up my face and couldn't look.
She, deep in grief, was more than grace.
I stayed a hideous, blank, and tight–shut book.

Eclectic forces drawing us apart;
Ecliptic natures bidding us to close;
Unfathomed faces windowed on the heart;
And yearnings, still, for one small full–blown rose.

New Mexico Memory

I couldn't know how a body blanches
once flung high up by the impact
of a speeding car, and Life retreats.
Or how groceries, hair, and clothing
scatter and form surreal patterns
on the shoulder's grassy mat.
Or how that strong man would gag
and swerve at sight of the white form.

It was not his doing, and he didn't stop.
"Enough gawkers here," he muttered,
then drove with an unreal slowness
all that long way into Demming, as he mopped
at the icy drops upon his forehead.

On the way back to Columbus he stared
straight to center when we passed the spot,
(without the body now, but recognized),
while I saw an image of the old one's pure snow body
forever in chalk graffiti on the pavement.

That white, white skin still flashes
to me sometimes, yet, years after;
and I think that there would be
red, sun–bleached plastic roses
by that roadside now. And a wooden cross.
I will not go up again from Columbus
on that flat straight road to Demming.

At Loss

Those who have come out of the fog
and mists of what Death did —
perhaps drifting out at random,
having spent much time in those
turgid backwaters and swamps of grief —
have a lot to tell us.

Except that they've come to know enough,
by their drop by drop bleeding,
that they must never tell anyone
that such is so, nor would they be believed.

Calmness, then, and platitudes
are all their dry eyes advise
and lips impart, else days wouldn't pass.
Else the monumental impact of it take us.
Else we believe we can learn to navigate
through the deep of waters ever unknown.
If ever there were charts and maps,
they've been burned or kindly hidden
by those compassionate mourners
who went before us on those waters.

Stones Can Cry Out

Spoken words can't say it to me at this stage,
so I sit amid a blank, unthinking silence
and know again the accomplishment of waiting.

Even music that might waft me off and far
most times won't work for me here
It's too much surety to think in tune.

Some peace falls down at once on me
because I know I do not know.
Now doubt can blend with hope in harmony.

Not for me the arrogance of certainty
when face to face with an All–Knowing.
What testament can I give save silent presence?

Lanier's Glynn Marshes aren't for me
in this old age that's come to seek me out.
I believe, for this one day, at least,
I'll choose to die in Simple Wonder.

Rain

I had not felt rain
that stung, or burned, or caused me pain.
My childhood dampenings
were soft and blurred
or happily pell mell with summer laughing.

I'd eagerly turned
to face rain's strident slap
as a challenge to how alive I felt.
Whooping and open–faced,
I splashed barefoot and aware.
Even that wild spring flood
meant canoe rides on the lawn.

But just now, as I knelt beside the grave,
in summer heat as warm as childhood's memory,
rain came to flail and pelt and gouge at me.
It beat and lashed and violently fought,
till, fetal–shaped, I curled and cried.
I may not ever trust a rain again.

Disinterment

I buried him.
For years in my heart's depths he's lain —
not quite rotting,
for it's not the same as when death and nature
take your love.
The earth I covered him with
was careless, loose, sun–flecked
forgetfulness.

But now and then
the sun's cloud–hidden.
His face, his gestures rise to me
unbidden, and I realize that, after all,
he's not too deeply laid.

A voice like his
may be the spade that cuts
into the humus of my mind.
And then I find all my thoughtless Lethe
dissolving
into sharp, sweet stabs of memory.

I Weep

for the loss of the things not remembered,
and I cry over moments I cannot recall.

If all we are left with are memories,
then the oldest are richest, by far,
even if those we shared them with are gone.
But counting all my memories in these shaded
older days doesn't occupy me all the time,
and so many years are merely shadows now.

So I weep for the loss of things not remembered,
and I cry over moments I cannot recall.

But the big fear, the big dread,
that which drives us to say that we
may give Kevorkian a call, is that
almost unspeakable horror, to be damned:
to never remember at all.

That Timed Path

comes ticking out of a youth
too thoughtless to know it's fleeting.
That timed path
comes down aisles of wondering,
through miles of vast uncertainties
where decisions weigh
with the heaviness
of gods on thrones.

Yet always, ever, in the back of it,
the knowing they will live forever.
This one day they reckon with
will be followed decisively,
whether they will or no, by the next
down That Timed Path.

But some hand turned the timer
and allowed them just so long,
no longer, before the buzzer goes.
Then it's all up, every second done,
down That Timed Path.

In Mourning

I wear self–conscious black
A bright songbird which can no longer bear
the sound of song.
A bud which cannot tolerate spring sun,
I've been asleep too long.

I've been in soft dusk, or in candle glow,
and suddenly cringe when dark's electrified.
An orchid snatched from its jungle lush
and thrust into dry desert sand
because she died.

All things have shades of meaning, or of light.
She too has a shade which clings to me.
The shock, the surging sense of loss.
The ultimately cruel floating free.
A Siamese twin, from whom they've cut
the other half of me.

On That Day

In night ink
Let me pass to Mystery
Without a man–made light
To hold me here
Or show me leaving.
Harsh birth–trauma
Brought me out
To glaring knowing,
But I would pass
On to beauty's Mystery
In darkness, wrapped simply
In its peace.

Her Brothers

One, the age of her oldest child,
and always to her as much child as sibling,
was cut by polio's scourge
to a life of pain and lameness.

Two went to war.
Her most beloved,
shot down and strafed in Burma,
sleeps in Hawaiian grave.
She finally ascertained this for herself
with a journey and a photo.
That brought her a long–sought comfort.

The other one, telegrapher,
went to Germany from England
50 bombing missions, earning home leave.
When he stayed then a month with us,
his screams of terror rent the nights.

Last brother, oldest, lives still
at age of 90 on a farm he helped
his son to work into old age.
His days are filled now quietly
with crosswords and jigsaws
and efforts at remembering.

Dear Annie,

I miss you,
Miss how you breezed in and out of my life.
Suddenly, breaking months or years of silence,
You were there, wanting to take me to lunch.
We'd empty pot after pot of tea,
And never play catch–up at all.

I miss you,
Seething with understatement,
Full of original cliches I'll quote the rest of my life.
I miss my fond jealousy of your so apt put–downs.
Miss your subdued (or were they
Really superstitious?) appreciations.

I miss
Arguing with you until five A.M.,
My first exposure to both blistering sarcasm
And sweet logic, your left hand gesturing,
Your sure voice mastering
Boldly every conversation.
You could argue for the saints
Or for the Devil himself with equal clarity.

I miss
My admission at being unequal to your wit.
I miss your drollness even on the rare occasions
When you complained. I miss our friendship
That should have gone on till ninety–five,
Cut off at least thirty years too soon.

I miss
Not being able to weep with you at your death.
You'd have known how to console me.
Typically, my last word from you was the
Easter card you sent me in January.
I miss your spunky faith
So un–at–home in the real world.
I miss you, Annie,
And, besides, I owe you lunch.

O Oregon!

It's been more than a decade now
since I first aged and ached my eyes
on clearcut wreckage.
Now I'm back and see the hillsides
have managed to cover up
some shame by springing forth
sheets of speckled foxgloves
in decorator colors.

Why do I feel it's only interim
kindness? The hillsides' nudity,
even in fresh printed sheets, appalls.

The Lorax and the Druids
and the Earth First! huggers
all left urgent messages on our
answering machines,
heard enough by frantic user
exploitation to hide the miles
and miles of trains,
(heaped with the dust of tree corpse,
destined to be shipped to islands
where trees–grown–in–cups is art form),
hide them from the highways
to compensate the tourists
by buffer zones of proud giant trees,
that once dressed all these hills.

Small Farm Death

Into the bright
hot April night
a February moon shone
his father's ghost.

No crops got planted
while he yet mourned
away another season.

He'd made promises
he couldn't keep
about carrying on.
He knew he'd take
his father's ghost
on the road with him.

The abandoned, wondrous fields
would sigh and wrap
uselessness around themselves,
a memorial mantle.

Later, a housing development
or mall corporation
would twist the knife.

Monuments

Perhaps, in the end, nature, and God,
will decide we aren't worth keeping,
we wasters and spoilers of earth's gifts.
We may be worth nothing more than
those who made the Easter Island forms,
worth no more than the pyramid–makers,
with jungles quietly reclaiming, reclaiming,
with deserts shifting their heavy sand burden.

By lack of understanding, and of care,
(technologies are no help at all with these),
we may sink deeper into oblivion, further
hid beneath the flowers, the seas, the sands,
further even than those other once–inhabitants.
Nature's common sense may shrug us off
and gladly prove that we were nobodies.

Anyone or Thing looking back
may find it difficult to know us.
Dollar–stores, internet, ice cream cones
and $200 sneakers notwithstanding —
we may at last be invisible and silent.
For we are grown too numerous and too
uncaring of each other, and of this earth.

Will our sad, tragic governments, with
their greedy, smug, irrational decisions,
keep up their wars and flaunt their bombs
'til there's not one person left to tell?
Will our proud monuments then be, logically,
oil derricks, cooling towers and missiles?

Political Repercussions

Eden Remembered

Excalibur came out of the stone to meet me.
It was that time, at eighteen years as I recall,
when my own power
was equal to the task.
In depths of quiet meditation
the world would fall into my lap
and look adoringly up at me.

Good thing, you say, those times don't last,
How would it be
if the love and power unbound
and the knowledge without limit
of all the eighteen–year olds
in all the world around
were both unleashed and lasting?

Cities might not get built.
Things not get produced.
Roads and factories and markets
not even dreamed of!
Why, wars might not get started,
guns not even invented.
How would that be?

It would be all just Wonder,
Mystic Music, Poetry and Laughter!
Art created with no thought of sales.
Mountains allowed their grandeur
without forestry or mining,
so the spirits of the createds could freely
roam and speak to eighteen–year–olds
who could weep, and paint,
or write a poem, or just love life
while they caressed those worlds
newly fallen onto their laps.

I Live My Days in Overmourn

for I didn't know, back when life was busier,
and happiness for granted, that one day
for many days I'd be stuck so in this gear.

And there's so much to weep for!
The very gaudy well–worn opulence
of it impresses and depresses me,
pulls me to its level,
nearly drowns me in its seas.

At fault or not, the guilt of everyman
(not equally shared, for those who cause
most mourning probably feel not guilt,
but pain) wounds and wounds and wounds
and yet does not quite kill.
What can be left to do but mourn?

Somewhere

Ladies still wear bright colored dresses with self–material belts,
still polish white pumps for Sunday, and carry small and
immaculate white purses. They may have given up lace–edged
handkerchiefs for kleenex, but the white shoes and purse
begin on Memorial Day, and are always exchanged
the day after Labor Day for black or brown ones.
    But not in my world.

Somewhere children sit in little chairs in a circle
Under Salman's Head of Christ and memorize Bible verses,
then are rewarded for their parroting with small
Bible bookmarks on which are printed:
"Smile, Jesus Loves You" or "Jesus Wept".
    But not in my world.

Somewhere men climb into three–piece suits
and affix color–coordinated ties with tiny
expensive and religious stick pins, tuck Bibles
under arms or slide them into pockets,
and back carefully vacced and waxed Buicks out of garages.
    But not in my world.

Somewhere a teenaged girl at the organ plays
"Just As I Am" a full dozen times on Communion Sunday
as young and old adults shuffle forward.
Couples take turns holding babies and watching youngsters
so that all adults can partake.
    Only not in my world.

Somewhere collection plates on long poles groan
under the weight of pledge envelopes and cash.
On Missionary Sunday the second round of baskets
is loaded while the choir sings all the verses of
"In Christ There Is No East or West".
    Just not in my world.

The young missionary holds everyone entranced
for over an hour with stories of natives somewhere
yearning for the message of the Lord (and of democracy)
    But not now.
    Not here.
    Nowhere at all in my world.

Feminist

When life drifted gently, without purpose,
through her veins, she sat behind the fat
cabbage head, like a frightened frozen rabbit
and just watched.

For long lengths of time she couldn't move
or wouldn't draw forth an ambition to be
up and gone, or try to make any distance
from this lackluster.

But something happened as the shades
grew stretched and spectral. A memory of need
caused blood to surge and course.
Then she knew

that she breathed in and out, but more!
She knew this pulse to be as old as time,
recognized her need to go as deep as
her humanity.

She's up and running now, the race that she
was born for, hoping that she'll discover,
before time overtakes her, the reality of
her ancestral dreams.

Should Have Planted Cosmos Blues
October, 1988

Drought's got the potatoes, and likewise
    the sweet corn.
Can't seem to wake up to a soft
    and dewy morn.
The wool ain't been sold yet, but this poor lamb
    sure is shorn.
I know somehow I should have planted
    cosmos.

I sit lookin' out at life like through a brown and
    sun–fried haze.
This dog's seen one too many of them dang
    dog–gone dog days.
Lookin' to the east, they's always Fermi's
    red–eyed glaze.
I really think I should have planted
    cosmos.

This summer's had me payin' for my past life
    full of sin.
Humidity's caught up with the heat,
    its ugly twin.
And Jesse's out (me too), while Ronnie
    still is in.
Serves me right, I should have planted
    cosmos.

Guv'ment's up to nothin' but its normal
    foreign disgrace,
while at home they's roads and bridges out
just
    all over the whole place.
And I got poison ivy blisters acoverin' up
    my face.
Ah me, I should have planted
    cosmos.

Commissioner Kuron, 'gainst all odds, just got
    hisself beat.
A friend o' mine just cut me dead awalkin'
    down the street.
I needed that somehow to make my sorry
    life complete.
I just know now that I should have planted
    cosmos.

The Fortress

The Fortress
(a metaphor I do not like, but apt)
protects my sanity
from the headlines,
from the daily news.
How could I live
in the here and now
without my blank mind's kindness?

Sometimes the firestorm without is so vicious
I awake burned
and find a portion
of my fortress charred away.
This damage caused by headlines,
by the daily news.

But still I huddle,
a long–time, recovering,
badly–scarred survivor,
within my fortress
of the blankness of my mind.

Built–In Pardons

Jesus, forgive us,
for we know damned well what we do.
But all men are sinners
and You still love us all,
maybe even love us more
for the really bad stuff
that would make us
red with shame
if we didn't know that
"All men have sinned and fallen short".
Makes me feel a little proud
to be in Your God–defined all.

Well, so my houses are condemned
and some needed to be torn down
by the city. Wasn't I doing my part
to help the poor we have always
too damned much with us?
Wasn't I generous to them
to only charge $600 when
others would've charged 'em eight?
Wasn't I helping out when I took in
that fellow off the street?
Shows how right I was
when he thanked me by burning
down the house one night.
Made a fire in the bedroom
out of wood from the living room.

He said to keep warm, but
I'm the one out the $600 monthly
welfare check. I always ask myself
before stepping in to help someone,
"Now, what would Jesus do?"
Look at the thanks I get.

..., Stock and Barrel

Can anything be more at odds with life
than a door that's locked?
When it's my own, I've either lost my keys
or locked them safe away inside.
When it's another's, it tells me
he won't trust a civilized approach
with proper knock, then waiting calmly
to be asked (or not) to enter.

I think the breakdown of the whole world
started with the very first lock.
Proceeded, then, with a grinding
and an exponential malice, to the holders
of the locks to their own keys. They have
the means to grant or block all entrances —
to an education, to a job, a meal, a life.
So seekers all must bow and scrape
and beg and lose to grovel all that love of self
and freedom that makes a human human.

I don't want a key, or set of them,
to drag about and pull me down as fetter.
I don't want a lock to call my own,
thus keeping me aloof, with the choice
to care or not left to my discretion,
my very charity (read: love), left up to my greed.

I want a lockless world!
For what else is poor shackled Freedom?
Note that key and lock makers, holders,
call her many different names.
Make no mistake: there's great big bucks
in locks. Yet where all the keyless and the lockless
find safe habitat and welcome will be the only spot
fertile enough for the civilized to grow.

Oh Lord

Liberate Christmas from the hard–sell.
Deliver us from the glut of cheap
slave–labor junky gifts
that flood the stores
and do not say, "I love you."
Free us this holy day
from the frantic buying
that spoils our childrens'
souls with avarice.
The obscenity of too much
can never be worth the
thankfulness of just enough.
Not a Dicken's village this,
for wasn't his the "worst of times"?
Still, turn the Tim in us to power
and our Scrooge to blessing.
　　　Amen.

So... Cop a Plea

No mystery gifts please
no fun–in–the–sun
no giant giveaways
Tell it like it is and not
how you want me to perceive it.

Is it good for the natural world?
Would you feed it to babies?
Will it make my spiritual life more sublime?
Is it the same stuff that
the pres and the congress enjoy?
Could those 9 court jesters read
its PR and stay straight–faced?

Not everyone's a fool anymore
and those who have grown up from foolish
now know how to ask questions
now know when answers are lies.

I know I wouldn't want to be
today's questioned–authority.

There Sometime Was a Peace

about the mailman's visit.
"Like this weather, Mrs. S?"
or "How're the kids?" he'd say.
We'd chat a moment,
lightly talk of politics, or clouds,
or flowers that were abloom beside the door.

That was before,
when nothing much would come in any mailing:
    infrequent bills
    Aunt Libbie's cards
    or that single, longed–for garden catalog
    which brought us dreams of spring
    in living color.

But then all the merchants of the world
discovered mailmen, who'd do their selling
for them, at a tenth or less the cost.

As he struggles, over–laden,
'neath the burden of those pitchmen,
I find I feel too guilty
to engage in conversation such a busy,
harried worker bent on finishing his tasks.

I'm too ashamed to take his time to talk
or even ask about his family;
and I've lost the will to smile
as he hands me five pounds, rubber–banded.

"Junk mail" it's been branded,
so I guess that he's the junkman;
but how I miss my mailman,
and that leisure, and our talks.

Civilized

Closeted within the fitful guise of being civilized,
We've done god–awful things.
We've clipped the wings off butterflies,
taped up the throats of songbirds,
cut off the talons of the eagles,
and broke the teeth of lions and of sharks,
poured poisons on our own food
just to kill the weeds, the weeds
we might as easily have pulled,
had we not looked for, insisted on, our ease.
We've cut the largest of the trees, and watched
them waste the small ones as they fell.
The road to very Hell is paved by acts like these.

The more "civilized" our thinking, the more
barbarous our actions, 'til the very stones
must cry out for a vengeance on us all.
The tears of a creating God, at the pig sty
we've made His Eden, then must either
wash us clean or make us gone before His wrath!
Kicked off the path He made for us to follow,
ungrateful, minute gnats, we'll burn away
in microseconds, leave not one spark
to witness we were here once, here,
in technocratic glory, "civilized".

Guilt by Association
in memory of Paul Wellstone

I may not like the concept,
but I have worked with grapes.
I know good buddies on the vine,
each pressing close to each,
when there's a worm involved,
spell disaster for the crop,
that one–bad–apple thing.

And, too, when two or more grapes
grow together but separate, and
free and strong, each in its own
space, no room is left for worms.

Worms are involved in politics:
twin worms of greed and lust,
and the daddy worm of power.
When you add the fat worms of
blind obescience to a church
or state, the whole wide world,
grapes and all, is in trouble.

Find me a man (or woman)
who cannot be bought, the one
to whom the price of worms
is just too high, and I'll say, "Lead!"

We may all have worms, that
writhe and tempt within our gut,
but to give our whole selves over
to such spoilage mars our soul.

The juice and jelly that sparkles
on the shelves, untainted by the
worms, is like a true and rare
democracy, its purity and loyalty
to its aims worth more than arms
or added territory, its citizens
happily envied by the world.

I Could Be a Hermit

and be tucked into a cave or shell most times,
seeming oblivious, yet contemplating, in any more years given,
the injustices I'd seen, raising resolute prayers
against weapon–based cultures,
against destruction–driven societies.

In the ages now called "dark" such were known,
in European Christendom as in far east antiquity,
and were not blamed if they shunned for love
those whom they loved, to sit aside, and give utmost intensity
to their prayers, as with a knife cut off from the world
and from its dear and all too human distractions.

Enlightenment must come to each dark age.
Can this one's only be when many weep and worry alone
about the darkness, and cut themselves from all
communication save with the Source, Who may well
weep now in isolation that It wills not?
Who sobs because its children miss Its mother's milk,
unknowing, as they scorn Its father's guiding hand!

Traditional prayers, even if shouted out in church,
cannot restore to us Her sweet breast. Old hymns,
even if sung by great professional choirs,
cannot regain His loving governance, even if we would.
We're now a people who've foresworn tradition.
By incising all that held us to sincerity and pain,
in our races to great riches, by our real fears that
others' sustenance may cut into our profits, we now find
ourselves with nothing in our headlong rush to have it all.

How can we rearrange our aims and prayers?
How praise the One when we just keep destroying
all that It made that we would praise It for?
How can we offer thanks, yet keep abusing
those blessings and those beauties we give thanks for?
How dare we petition when we have so very much,
yet doublespeak simple sharing as injustice?
For now, my hermitage must be all penitential:

Mea culpa, Mitch Snyder, for I have two coats and more.
Mea culpa, Woody, for I've let the unions
let us down, and refused to heed your songs.
Mea culpa, native peoples, for I've helped push you
onto bleak, drugged, dependent homelessness;
Then helped the poor in desolate cities be the same.
Mea culpa, Iraqi Kurds, for I tempted you to hopes
I can't and won't (and really never intended to) fulfill.
Mea culpa, Queen Alexandra's Birdwing, for with my greed
I'm now plotting your extinction, and, given time,
that of all your kind; 'til only I and mine remain.
Mea culpa, Earth, for I have taken, taken, taken
with no thought of giving back!

Of Value

They say it's just a weed, but worse,
the purple loosestrife filling up the marshes
where the wild ducks used to feed.
The worse because it gives no food for duck or hunter
while crowding out the cattail, food for man and duck.
And yet, it must be flowering out of some wise plan.
May not lovely purple spike enrich my eye
as gunshots thrill a hunter's ear?

They've declared war on the catbird
who fills the nest of "wanted" songbird, and then leaves,
its bigger babe a hardship on the smaller bird who stays and feeds,
and sees its own young starved out in the process.
And yet, the cowbird doesn't even know the way to build a nest!
Is she responsible for her natural ignorance?

They say they're lower class, embarrassing, and threatening
to the tourist trade, the gamins filling up the streets
of Rome and Rio, Paris and Detroit, young boys and prostitutes.
Some are allowed to shoot each other, or run drugs ,
or satisfy the "prurient interests" of the moneyed class.
Some, in periodic "cleansings," are run off, or shot off,
of the streets, as rats might be, or simply gathered into jails,
or, if convenient, "disappeared," when an international
conference comes to town, like recently in Rio.

What of the loosestrife, catbird, street life? Who are we to say
the One whose eye is on the sparrow's not on them?

Peace with Justice

Justice walks with Peace.
He is her fierce defender.
She's delicate and shy;
she'd never make it on her own.
He precedes her by a few steps,
as he tells her story, how she cannot
go anyplace without him.
If they want to make her acquaintance,
they must first pass his inspection.

When they reach his goal,
you'll find that she's there too.
They'll make a splendid marriage,
Sir Justice and Lady Peace,
always caring for each other,
always wanting only the best.
We'll all dance at their wedding,
a marriage surely made in Heaven.

Off–Camera O. J. Questions
and the Death Penalty

Why would women want somebody dead
if he'd beaten and killed a woman?
Is their ambition equality of hate?
Have they dominant–male–retribution syndrome?
Who would they blame if they were the abusers?
Have they felt under so long
they'd turn dogs just to come out on top?

I had hoped feminism wasn't, after all,
about winning or besting or showing up.
"Take up your cross," we were told,
men and women alike, not "Crucify Romans."
I had hoped that feminists had learned more about females
than so–called Christians ever learned about Christ.

To Mr. Clinton
June 26

There is a picture that I cherished in my mind
of you and your mother, holding hands, faces rich with delight,
jumping off your porch steps, after your election was a
certainty. Your own delightful Camelot! And our own,
for we were born with you. You seemed to gather up
and hold aloft our hopes for the future: goodness,
salvation of Nature's gifts to us, a better world.

And again we felt reborn that you chose a poetess to speak.
Woman! Poet! Her voice warm with the hope we felt.
Her voice which held back the echo of "smart bombs".
Her voice hallowed with the import of Death's other.
Her voice which slid healing hands over the recent wounds
of the killing and the killed, even over the egotistic U! S! A!

Now you stand shifty–eyed before us. I read between your words
the military line: "Let this be a warning. Our Rome
will not be interfered with, and this bombing's a reminder
that we have the biggest guns with which to rape the world.
Democrats, Republicans, no difference. You must remember
    We are now the only Superpower!"

I see the military/industrial snarl transform your lips,
lips that had seemed vulnerable. That image smashes ugly
against that so–human mind picture that I treasured,
that picture of youthful and spontaneous joy that had lit you
when you leaped from the steps with your mother.
All this while my hopes search wildly, frantically, looking
for a different, better bearer of them — for the next time.

November, '94

The returns start their flow,
and I snap off the radio.
I don't want to hear that a Bush or a North
is again loose and at large.

Oh yes, I know of the trusts
that are broken on both sides;
and the N. P. P. and the Greens
haven't a Hell's snowball's chance.

But it's HUMAN to hang onto hope,
and Hope was that Arkansas town
whose son caught our hearts
like a brilliant intercept on the field.

But we watched in stunned silence
as he smiled and he wept,
then still carried that ball, clutched tight,
toward the enemy's goal post.

Now I realize what all of them fear.
Both parties hate what we cling to as ours.
A people hoping and free, their one true enemy;
and they'll make any deal to kill these.

Political Repercussions

Classes, in the Day of the Newts

How far can my plebeian fancy take me?
Only just as far as your patrician mind suggests.

For while you hold all purse strings,
I must always dance your dance;
and while you hold the office
it would seem that you know best.

All I'm actually guaranteed
is what you feel like granting.
Just tell me what you say I need,
and I'll go steal the rest.

My baby's hungry, and you begrudge me pennies.
Your baby steals my baby's milk and shoes and dress.

Slipping Through

They hadn't a chance now of making do.
Though the wolf had cried before
and been pacified, it had been less hungry.
Now all the concessions had been made.

Savings, once withdrawn, just couldn't be returned,
until the slim book stood at zero.
Food cut. All meat went first.
Finally just apples and cheap white bread.
They were glad that their little boy,
stillborn, wouldn't have to starve.

Tonight they'd walked the market round
for hours, smilingly accepting samples,
drinking down many mini cups
of free and fancy coffees, heavy with
powdered cream and several sugars.

She suggested, when the stores closed up
that night, that they not return to those
three empty rented rooms with irate landlord.
That they look no more on the bills for
cancelled phone, heat, lights, and water.

"It's lovely now down by the water at night,
all Christmassy where the snow blows
white around the street lights. Let's go
take a walk there now. We can stop, and sing
to our baby who's waiting for us.
It may well be the easiest thing we've done,
to slip down gently between the cracks,
and hold each other until it's done.
I wonder who might notice that we've gone."

Rescued or Taken November 25

As the international story grew,
a small boy was feted with Disney.
Could the world's most expensive pretend —
its rides and bright lights —
compensate, some way,
for lost mother, lost home?

His small arms nearly pulled
from their sockets by politics
(no little child should have to
bear the creed or wear the crud of politics),
prayers, speeches, posturings and lawsuits
wash about him like the ocean
where he lost her.

But doesn't he have a pillow to cry in?
Hasn't he been given a promise
of whatever others claim is a "better life"?
Worldwide flogging of a giant power
pitted against a little nation lost in
its own little power and self–defense,
ideologies have trampled on humanity,
with countrymen, kinsmen and strangers
all battling for his keep.

But what of you, little Elian?
(sadly ironic, your homonym name)
Who speaks of your dreams?
Who knows of your nightmares?

To Feed the World

He weeded with his pocket knife,
hacking viciously in anger at usurpers,
cursing them with all manner of threats,
using a powered spader between neat rows,
promising, in frustration, the use of Round Up.

She weeded, bare–handed, in the dirt,
talking to her plants,
admonishing the weeds to "stay out there"
beyond her flowers' reach.
She gently cut back dead stalks
and apologized to the overgrowth while thinning.

He slashed and pruned,
driven by ambition.
She mulched and crooned,
gave no thought to profit.

"Mine is the better way," he said,
"if all are to be fed."

"If each fed just his own,
then freely gave of surplus,
our unpoisoned earth would blossom,"
she retorted.

He harvested trailer loads of produce,
bragged of what he sold at market,
vowing next year to put more acreage to truck.
She brought inside each day` an apronful
for the evening meal, grateful for enough.

Terminator Seeds

The corporations that gave her body cancer
had years ago planted terminator seeds:
death–chemicals and radioactivity.
Now they have done their worst,
and she will not reproduce.
Nor, with her own health so precarious,
can she even hope to adopt.

The god Profit has melded into madness
the big Ag monsters and maniacal Chem giants.
What chance do little people have
of growing food to raise their families?
What chance to have a family at all?
What chance does blessed biodiversity
have to survive this ugliest of onslaughts?

We used to sing of a God who'd made
all things to perfection (whether it was
instantaneous or by eons of change,
we trusted a Creator.) But could there be
an evil enough hideous ogre to have made
the one who first thought of terminator seeds?

Linda Lay, Distraught

She's had to go and open up a shop,
forced into such a lowly business
by circumstances few of us could fathom:
Imagine! To be left with just one residence!
(The homeless and the working poor,
if they could afford the paper or a radio,
would click their tongues in sympathy.)
It's just wretched when you've climbed
up those damned turtles' backs to find
that you've slipped off (along with all of them).

But don't go there thinking it's a garage sale,
something like the rest of us would have.
This lady's weeping 'cause she's selling treasures
expects to get a queen's ransom for her pains.
But the nouveau riche we've always with us;
your wealth is old stuff now — get over it.
Bite the bullet and eat cake, poor Linda Lay,
for you probably once owned the bakery.

Zero Tolerance

A single solitary slip–up is more than they'll abide.
Just one and out; you can't make more than one.
They call it "zero tolerance", those cats that know to hide
all the really, really bad things that they've done.

"Collateral damage"? Expect it in war, they say.
Our bombs are smart, so there's really little of it.
But if just one civilian got in just one smart bomb's way,
by your rule you should take your war and shove it!

A gradeschool kid's expelled for not doing what he ought.
Out the door; there can be no substitution.
But grown–ups running Enron only cry if they get caught;
and who knows if there'll be any restitution.

Dirty politics has brought good runners to their knees;
while on–the–takers always seem to win.
This language–twisting leads to almost anything they please.
and if you're a churchman, only other people sin.

New Anthem of the Defeated

Oh Corporate America, we pledge to thee
Our lives, our blood and our most sacred dollar.
You lurk behind that tarnished flag
That our forefathers bled for.
You take your money off–shore
To avoid your country's taxes,
Taxes every little man must pay
For those wars waged for your sake.
You prostitute the very word of freedom.

You make our representatives rich
So they make laws in your favor.
You lure investor's coin into
Worthless, "name–only" savings
That will add more to your coffers.
You pay enough to elect your man,
Even as president. He becomes
The most powerful man on earth
So he can rule for you with impunity.

You buy the air waves up,
Air that the people own, and need
For their priceless liberty.
You buy up all the largest press,
Make huge cities one–paper towns
To help dispense with diverse opinions.

All these sell the goods that make you
Even richer, sell your point of view,
Even sell the so–called "news"
That we peons believe is true,
So we'll all kneel down and bow to you
And forever pledge U! S! A!

Questions for George V

So, who's the Court Jester
of this monarch's reign?
You're all so dead serious
you give me a pain.
There's naught said or done
for a smile or a grin.
Everything that you touch
is so deadly it's sin.

I want so to laugh again,
crow with delight;
but your lies give me headaches,
your bombs pierce the night.
It's just: buy, wear a flag,
and, oh yes, pay your tax,
or we can't keep our claws
in those terrorists' backs.

(At least Bill played the sax.)

So, who's the Court Jester?
Where's the comic relief?
You've stolen the office,
stand for "Hail to the Chief".
You've bloodied the world,
are out looking for more
poor folks you can slaughter
in your next brand "new" war.

But when can we laugh again?
When dance and sing?
O simpering imposter,
O marionette king.

for Bush, God and Media

Are there so few in this benighted land
whose understanding of our native tongue
is of such low degree that most can't see
the lies? Can't know deception and rank power
make mockery of this rich language?

Even so–called 'public' media walks the walk.
The *news* is blared at us without a seeming end
because such parroting's been bought and paid for,
while BBC's clipped, unemotional reports
seem to lend credence to uneducated ears.

I see, as Orwell saw, as Margaret Atwood feared,
we are defeated by the very language
they all twist to their advantage. But it's
the believers, as his backers, most deceived:
they think such politics will bring them,
and their puny knowledge, rapturing to their god!

Aftermath
October 1, 2002

The flags they hung from
    every light are filthy now.
Has patriotic fervor slacked,
    or drummed–up nationalism paled?
War and all war's rumors
    fill the air waves and TV.
They just don't get it that
    war means that all have failed.
No one takes down the flags
    to wash them clean again.
No one can wash our foolish
    nuclear–posturing away.
We end this season threatening
    the sweet world of green.
We end as we began it, with
    more people out of work, and
no one holds the terrorists at bay.

Now those who hold the power
    of those offices they stole
use all they have to threaten more.
    They crave and covet all–out war.
Economic slump? A war can cure it.
    Suspicions of the office?
A big war will take all that away.
    Ah, Daddy will be proud,
and the rest must just endure it.

Those who do not speak for us
    hold to their fear and nurse it.
They cannot, will not admit
    that we may have some blame.
"God Bless America", some faded
    yard signs still proclaim.
But what about the world?
    Are we asking Him to curse it?

Overheard from Another Room
April, 2002

Ah, darling, how I love you...
You knew I had to come
back here and kill you...
for as little as $19.99, plus postage...
That's the world today...
Lose 30 pounds in 30 days...
to preserve democracy...
Another shooting on the east side...
and get another one free...
Toledo Mud Hens hold their own...
with the accident on the expressway...
Protesters claim Yucca Mountain
is an unsafe place for nuclear waste...
Could it be that Israel is ready
to talk peace?... Another bombing...
Puts the bright back in your colors...
For that special one give flowers...
hints of torture in the prisons...
held a closed–door session...

Mainstream media soundbites
are revealing, and the remote control,
as always, is in another's hands.

No Nukes!

Nuclear Anything: 1982

I had dreamed,
(and woke in sweat and fear
and dragged myself about
with terror–laden eyes all day)
that the worst to come had:

Our government we'd so tentatively borne,
brought forth in pain and love,
had, like the offspring of Lear,
turned to vipers at our breast
and sold us to the enemy.

Eight laughable days of warnings,
mixed up with Edison's evacuation plans,
stupid words like "limited" and "safe",
sad, sad impossibilities beyond our fathoming.

First strike had flown through
the closest vulnerable window
and clashed with that other fear,
the enemy, our bastard son:
the logic of nuclear imbricate.

Faceless horsemen, apocryphal or real,
had trampled melting children underfoot,
while my ears could not dislodge or forget
an endless human scream,
a purgatorial Tenebrae forever,
but with no hope of Easter.

But worse, far worse, living past the nightmare,
the artery, pulse, and life–blood of the dream,
the beat of the tormented and tormenting vision:
    We could have done something.
    We should have spoken out.
    We didn't have to let this happen.

Simple Pleasures Stolen

I wish the sun's rise wasn't east,
or that I weren't west of Fermi,
or there were no nukes at all
to spoil my morning view.
Hope's dashed again each dawn
I wake to see it there.

But my poor friends
across the lake in Canada
have ruined sunsets.

First Do No Harm

for Mary Kate

There is no "away", and can be no disposing.
Our actual risks they're fearful of disclosing,
but on innocent lives they keep on foreclosing
in their evil haste to make more nuclear hay.

Dentists and doctors (unaware?) are misusing
their prime promise to Life, and, by this, are confusing
threats with hopes and with liberty–of–choosing.
And the nuke plants keep up their hellish fusing,
giving us death and disease when we get in their way.

Give us, at the very least, a smoker's chance!
Let there be published labels, so at a glance
we can discern how much poison that they feed us —
in food and water, soil and air, and each x–ray.

Vigil, January 27, 1987
for Barb LaBelle

One counts, and two is a quorum,
'cause if you ain't against 'em,
It looks like you're for 'em.
(You gotta think positive)

If eight show up on a darkened square,
Just think of the millions each represents there.
(Think Big)

If eight hold candles on a January night,
That's eight times nothin' to send out the light.
(But think Bright)

There was a fella spoke to a handful o' folk.
He told 'em He was the Light, and it wasn't no joke.
(Think BRIGHT)

He said a lot of things to that little composite,
Like if they weren't with Him, they were the opposite.
(Think Big)

He kept on sayin' things like Love is the key,
And keep on bein' true, 'cause Truth will set you free.
(Think Freedom)

One counts, and two is a quorum,
'Cause if you ain't against 'em,
It looks like you're for 'em.
(Think about it)

Last Season's Song

Shall I sue them for my loss of innocence,
which, once torn asunder, can never regrow?
    For I know too much to play in the snow,
    to innocently play in the snow.

May I sue for loss of joie de vivre?
It's gone, but tell me, where did it go?
    I just know too much to play in the snow,
    to innocently play in the snow.

My children, seeing flurries, chortle and crow,
and, though snowmen call, I still must say, "No."
    I must teach them not to play in the snow,
    not to innocently play in the snow.

I've heard it said that ignorance is bliss,
but in atomic times, not–knowing is the kiss
of death; and the number of sad eyes will grow
with the coming of the rain and the snow.

Time was when I rejoiced to feel the rain,
never thinking cancer, acid, poison, or pain.
    But now I know too much to play in the snow,
    to innocently play in the snow.

On the isles we spoiled the fallout ash was snow.
Children played and laughed there at ground zero.
    Now they know they must'nt play in the snow,
    Mustn't innocently play in the snow.

At Mount Hood, Swiss Alps, and Aspen slopes,
where they ski and frolic, faces all aglow,
    will they learn too much to play in the snow,
    to innocently play in the snow?

Transuranics come, they say, and transuranics go;
But slow they go, my friends. They die exceeding slow.
    Will we ever get to play in the snow,
    get to innocently play in the snow?

No Nuke

Cyclops

Nuclear physicist "twiddles" beneath his Cyclopean eye.
The people are there in the middle,
'Tween radioactive water and sky.
The natives are all getting restless,
As he kills us so softly with words.
His protestations range all the way
From the ridiculous to the absurd.
Policemen crowd every corridor,
'Cause we're really a scary bunch.
But we still don't want Fermi's water to drink,
Or its fish to eat for lunch!

Nanogram notes on the noninformational meeting at Cantrick School, Monroe, Michigan, Feb. 23, 1994, just before Edison dumped on us (again!), the night a bunch of kids' chants and signs had all of Monroe officialdom scared shitless.

Dedicated to (the memory of) a certain U. of M. professor of nuclear engineering, who shall remain nameless.

Songbook for Anti-Nukes (not to be confused with Christmas Carols)

Undeck the Halls

Undeck the halls from nuclear folly
Folly, folly la! La, la, la, la!
With no nukes at all we'd all feel jolly
Folly, folly la! La, la, la, la!
Enbrittled plants! Untested waste casks!
Folly la! Folly la! La, la, la!
"Where's the safety?" that's what we ask
Folly, folly la! La, la, la, la!

See that hot, hot waste before us
Folly, folly la! La, la, la, la!
"Stop the production!" must be our chorus
Folly, folly la! La, la, la, la!
Proper hearings! Public choices!
Folly la! Folly la! La, la, la!
Speak out now, while we still have voices!
Folly, folly la! La, la, la, la!

They picked Yucca Mountain, call it government land
Folly, folly la! La, la, la, la!
If it ever kept its treaties, it would be something grand
Folly, folly la! La, la, la, la!
Traveling nuke waste's not the answer
Folly la! Folly la! La, la, la!
Unless their intent is to spread more cancer
Folly, folly la! La, la, la, la!

Santa Claus Ain't Comin'

There's somethin' you can't see
Somethin' you can't smell
Somethin' you can't taste
But it's deadly as hell!
That's why Santa Claus ain't comin' to town.

He's struck off his list
All the nuclear dumps
'Cause radiation's worse
Than measles and mumps.
That's why Santa Claus ain't comin' to town.

Nuclear power makes it tough to remain here,
In an atmosphere of gloom;
And Santa's afraid to expose his reindeer
To the radiation doom.

So write your Attorney General
And your congressmen too.
Tell 'em radioactivity
Ain't no good for you,
And that's why Santa Claus ain't comin' to town!

Old Chestnuts

Old chestnuts that we have been sold before,
Like "Nuclear power's the way to go,"
All those lies that we've been told before —
All these are just a job of snow.

They say their power's safe, and not to sweat,
Or that we can get away okay.
The bets are on, but it's our lives they bet,
As the NRC looks the other way.

They think that they will still get by
With telling lies, and we will never question why.
But every mother's child one day will see
Through all those lies that once fooled you and me.

"Temporary" storage has a whole new meaning now:
It's permanent as it can be.
A "Drive–by" glance stands for close screening now,
At 18 feet up, a cinch to see!

Everybody knows Chernobyl isn't over yet,
and it could happen in this town.
There was Fermi I, Three Mile Island,
So, in case we forget, for a Merry Christmas
Shut It Down!

Nuclear–Plundered Land

Sirens blow! Do you hear them?
Do you know why we fear them?
They warn with a blast this day could be our last
'Cause we're walkin' in a nuclear–plundered land.

Gone away is the glad bird.
Here to stay is a sad bird.
He sings his last song, for songs can't last long
When you're walkin' in a nuclear–plundered land.

This big lake was once a summer treasure.
Families came from far and near to play.
Now with that poison fuel too hot to measure
They're chasin' all that family fun away.

Politicians say, "Just elect us."
You notice they won't protect us.
Don't stand there amazed; it's the public who pays
When we're walkin' in a nuclear–plundered land.

Green Christmas

The sun still shines, so why don't we use
its power to fuel our needs,
instead of ungodly fuel
that threatens our happy Yule?
But hope still lives in the human heart,
so this heartfelt wish I will now impart.

I'm dreaming of a green Christmas.
Safe solar power, unpoisoned lakes,
when we'll have no worries
of unleashed curies,
and the air is clean for all our sakes.

I'm dreaming of a green Christmas.
A time when we'll be given all our constitutional rights.
when our health and welfare,
not the nuclear industry's hell–fare,
comprise our elected officials' "lights".

I'm dreaming of a green Christmas,
a time when understanding will grow like you've never seen.
I'm confessin' Chernobyl's lesson, and I mean
to work 'til all our Christmases are green.

No Nukes

All We Want for Christmas

All we want for Christmas
Is some clean air to breathe,
Some unpoisoned food,
And a radiation–reprieve.
All we want for Christmas
Is to shut down this dump!
Then we could wish you, "Merry Christmas!"

It's been so long since we could say,
"The power's safe; the power's clean and healthy."
It's killing us, but we still have to pay
to make those nuclear suits wealthy.
So...

All we want for Christmas
Is some clean air to breathe,
Some unpoisoned food,
And a radiation–reprieve.
All we want for Christmas
Is to shut down these dumps.
Then we could wish you, "Merry Christmas!"

Rudolph

Rudolph, the red–nosed reindeer
has a very shiny nose;
and if you live around here,
you know exactly why it glows.

All of the other reindeer
don't want to get what Rudolph's got,
so they're catchin' the next sled out–a here
that goes to somewhere Fermi's not.

They had a fire on Christmas Day,
and a turbine missile too.
They've fixed it up now, or so they say,
but they can't fool me or you!

So Congress had better listen
and take a look at Rudolph's nose,
or the schnoz on that poor old Rudolph
won't be the only thing that glows!

There's No Place That's Safe

Oh there's no home here that's safe for the holidays
As long as Fermi Two sits by our lake.
If you want to be healthy in a million ways,
Get the NRC to shut down that mistake.

No, there's no place that's safe for the holidays —
Now that they're putting nuke waste out to roam.
If Congress wants to really mend its nasty ways,
It'll shut 'em all down, and keep its garbage home.

Jolly Old Saint Nicholas

Jolly Old Saint Nicholas,
do we have a prayer?
Bush's posture's first–strike nukes;
There's terror in the air!
He says he's getting rid of nukes
that clutter up the place
(But reserves the right to keep 'em
hidden, handy, "Just in case.")

He signed a treaty with
a former enemy of state.
As usual, he only does
too little, and too late.
But just in case you are relieved
and think you won't lose sleep,
just ask the Native Peoples:
How many treaties do we keep?

Up on the Housetop

Up on the Housetop reindeer die.
Please, Dear Santa, tell us why.
The same thing that poisoned the Lapland deer
Fermi could spit out at the dear folks here.

No, No, No! We shouldn't glow!
No, No, No! We shouldn't glow!
They poison our land and our air and lakes.
Nukes gotta go 'cause they're all mistakes!

First came the meltdown at Fermi one;
They didn't tell us so we couldn't run.
Then came all the snafus at Fermi two.
It was on Christmas Day that their turbine blew!

(repeat chorus)

When they tell us that a start–up's near,
Is it any wonder that we live in fear?
When they can't get it right, they repeat last year,
And that's about par for Fermi's Christmas cheer.

(repeat chorus)

O Nuclear–Free

O nuclear–free! O nuclear–free!
How beautiful that phrase is!
O nuclear–free! O nuclear–free!
We'll stand to sing its praises.

When nukes are gone
our hearts can sing.
No Nukes! will make
the rafters ring.

The phrase will spell true liberty,
and a better world will promise.
We want the whole wide world to be
nuclear powerless and bombless!

Our children will
be free to grow
without that fear
we had to know.

To rid the earth of all the nukes
must be our just endeavor.
Our prayer will be to keep it free
forever and forever.

Doom Drummer Song

Lies they tell us
    Da–doom Da–doom–doom
"They have no truth in them"
    Da–doom Da–doom–doom
They cover up the truth
    Da–doom Da–doom–doom
Why do they lie to us?
    Da–doom Da–doom–doom
    Doom–da–doom–doom
    Doom–da–doom–doom
Just for profit
    Da–doom Da–doom–doom
They'll be our doom

(Sing drum dooms after every *)

Native peoples*
Are told to take this waste*
Spit in their Mother's face*
Of Dignity, no trace*
So they can just make more*
To seal our doom

In our water*
They pour the stuff of death*
They poison fish and bird*
And what they do to them*
Is done to all of us*
They'll be our doom

In Our Time

The problems are much greater now
    than we had ever thought.
Guess we've come of age now,
    if we like it, or if not.
People cause all problems,
    their begat and their begot;
and it's people who must solve them
    in their time.

Folks won't take it like they used to,
    won't accept things as their lot.
Dr. Seuss's Yertle shows it's not
    too far to that top spot,
but if we climb the back's of others,
    someone else fills our poor slot.
We The People have to solve this
    in our time.

It's not that we can change it all,
    each tittle and each jot.
It's not that we can clean up
    every nuclear kilowatt.
But for our kids' sakes and our Earth's sake,
    we must give it our best shot;
for it's people who must do it
    in their time.

Governments are great for telling
    people what they ought,
except that they use cover–ups
    and lies and "just forgot".
Now those who love the Earth
    must tell the governments what's what,
'cause together we can do it
    in our time.

And, for God's sake! We're running out of time!

No Nukes!

Anti-War

New Math "Fact"

I am but six removed from you,
whoever you may be.
Chances are
(and it's all just chance)
we will never meet,
though we're family.

Related we are
by the ones between us,
whatever faces they wear;
and no one should ever
put asunder us and our
family care.

If government tries,
our brotherhood dies
in a war of land, race or nation;
so we must prove
we're just six removed,
and our brother is not an oblation.

I Cannot Go To Bed

with you," she said. "You've hands of gore."
He stared down at his hands
as though he'd never seen them quite before.
"It was a war," he said. "That's true,
but I fought in it for you."

"Not so!" she cried. "I never asked for death.
You never asked if you could kill for me!" she said.

"I'm marrying me the minstrel boy instead.
He went along with only harp and song.
And he'll spare my heart from pain
when your kind marches off to kill again.
His songs caress the truth, for
he full knows that without warriors
there never can be war."

Etymology, with Pain

Engagement:
fond and solemn promise
of a life together

or simple chatty stuff
of no great issue

or fierce and deadly
challenge of life's very tissue

Engaging:
said of flash of dimply cheek
or lively eye,
enough to make us
further seek such promise

or bloody meeting
on a fated far–flung ground
for purposes of murder
man–made legal

Engage:
to mesh the gears smoothly
so to move the vehicle on

or to meet some life
defined for you as enemy
and then tie up in combat
till you or he is gone

Ah, Elijah

All wars are the same,
at least to mothers.
all hells, alike:
from my mother's great uncle's
eighteen–year–old innocence
in that oxymoron Civil War
(what is civil about war?),
with his few short months
of coping and being brave
before his West Virginia death

down to the deadening
pornographic–driven sorties
of the Bush/Gulf killing
and to the very now of this, his son's,
terrifying "war on terrorists".

Generals and politicians use words
like "different" and "new",
but mothers know.
My great, great grandmother knew,
when Elijah at eighteen marched away —
no uniform, no gun, no preparation
(as if any of these could save him) —
She knew all wars are the same,
that all wars are hell.

Circa 1944, Whose War?

Vernors' Story

A fourth of my outfit lost, and all for what?
We were just fifteen left from the ship, with guns and gear.
I'd had it up to here with war and with this man's navy!
Three years, eleven months since I'd last seen home.

"Don't shoot the palm trees down. They belong to Palmolive."
But before I'd let that guy up there with a gun
blow my buddies away, I'd say, "The hell with Palmolive!"
Then blast away till both sniper and palm were rubble.

They sent us out on the strips with bushel baskets.
We were collection boys, and I don't mean church pews.
Here an arm, there a leg, next a shattered head. I stopped to vomit.
Drop a dog tag in on top, and ship someone home to Mother.

Time for me to go home; let some admiral replace me!
Bring the Big Shots out from Washington to finish their war.
A beefy Marine said he had no room for me and my fourteen.
I told him without our orders for home I'd blow him away.

(that's one thing about war, makes you not too choosy whose death,
your own, or his, or the enemy's, whoever that might be.)
And I meant what I said, and that Marine there knew that I meant it.
We would not give up our arms till we headed stateside.

So orders were issued while we sat there armed to the teeth.
The Marine had the final laugh, said, "Find your own way back!"
We hiked to the port, found a battered old merchant marine
that was three men short of a crew for the long haul home.

We went aboard, said we'd help 'em fight if need be.
We'd been navy men made for a patriotic cause,
then turned to rebels when our bellies had got their fill.
Twenty–five percent of my buddies dead for Palmolive Peet.

On the Care and Feeding Of

I can't forget a mother who told me that my childish
wrongs, large and small, hurt both her and me.
She scolded, then she hugged me to her heart,
She showed me, always, that love's the better part.
All faiths teach this; how could we have forgotten?

Both old and modern efforts made at making peace,
bragged about by industrial/military "statesmen",
will ever be in vain, if forgiven and forgot
can't come to play; if mothers are not honored
for the things they taught; if some foolish
notions of what makes a man or nation great, not
redefined. We work so hard at making pride
a good thing, yet it still heads the list of sins.
And, taken to extreme, it's ever spelled out
war and fratricide. True heroes work at problems
without guns, and change their greed to sharing.
Youths must be taught that killing just breeds killing.

To You, Private Ryan

If one lamb is lost, said the Good Shepherd,
leave the ninety–nine to find the one.

Red crosses on hats
White flashes
(Obscenities before a loving God)
Red blood
White sand
How many pints turn the waves to scarlet?
How many centuries of wars tint the very seas?
Medics needing medics
Voices of derision
from pages of unlearned history,
"Physician, heal thyself."

Flag folks can never comprehend
cowards with typewriters
(or, lacking these, valuing the stub of a pencil
nearly more than life itself);
yet from this journalism behind dead cows
came the staccato of rain drops emulating gun shots,
trading, momentarily, mud for blood.

Perhaps the only sanity was his who noted
that death–swiftness would not slow to flat reality,
that wave after wave of good dead men
both sides
saluted, as they died, their flags and politicians;
for thoughts of love and home must be
as deliberately denied as religion embraced
while they donned blood–filled helmets.
Sound blurs, and very reason lapses
as sacrifices pile up at Death's altar.

But who noted that Pilate won again,
by default, washed his hands again?
As we again made decisions well behind
general's stars, white hairs, closed doors
that whatever the young had died
and killed for had to be made to be worth it —
Let's go out and have ourselves a parade!

Cruel aftermaths must haunt those
generations who were not yet born,
those who will always only know D–Day
as an answer in a crossword puzzle.
Still, they'll carry DU from their own Bush War
to slyly poison them and their future sons.

So you, Private Ryan, catch and hold us all
with the taste of the penultimate pain of war:
the shame of now and future deaths.

Young Uncle

He screamed in the night as his war's nightmares shook him.
He'd seen the flames left by his bombs down below.
My mother said, "Patience. He's had a rough time,
and wars are so hard on the winners, you know;

and man's so inhuman to man."

My uncle was dear as a young uncle could be.
He played with us kids, and sang with his guitar.
Plucking a tooth from his comb as a pick,
he'd ask which songs we fancied, which tunes we would hear.

(I always picked out the ones with the yodeling,
but man's so inhuman to man.)

He'd flown fifty missions, was rotated home.
He stayed with our family a full month or so.
Like a small child (I thought), he took afternoon naps;
but would scream out and sob as day dreams overtook him

for man's so inhuman to man.

Life never got better for him after that.
He went back to the farm, but was restless and sad.
He just couldn't throw off his part in the bombings.
His family disowned him; it got bad as that.

All wars are inhuman to man.

Happy, sensitive man, red–haired and eyes twinkling,
he used to sit out on the front stoop and sing.
All his nephews and nieces would clamor around him.
His charms drew us like magnets. To his side we'd cling.

but war's so very inhuman to man!

It's not patriotic to protest this "new" war.
We were attacked, changes all things, can't we see?
It's okay to bomb them (though it's all they have known).
And my uncle's screams in his sleep still ring through me,

and man's still so inhuman to man.

What would it take now to wean us from the oil that
we so covet, worldwide, we wage war on the poor?
Will we grind with our warboots all nations that have it,
leaving rubble, dead horses and not a lot more?

We've been so inhuman to man.

How dare we to use the word "civilization"!
How dare we to speak out against theirs as we do!
When this one of ours is so greedy and evil,
we do unto others shouting "Red, White and Blue!"

Our war's so inhuman to man.

Wars are so damned important we study them daily.
We indoctrinate kids with them all the day long.
But look what we do to ourselves in the process,
making killers of uncles who used to sing songs.

Killing kills off the best part of man.

Unheard at the Peace Table

Shut up, my friend.
Our "sides" are well–defined
and too many miles apart to reconcile.
But if you sit there in that chair
and I sit here in mine,
we may arrive, sans words, at
a sort of commonality of being.

You there in the sun,
you there, shut up!
Don't say one word more.
Simply listen to my stillness
as I hear how you are without a voice.
Words always did create the fights,
and not just fighting words.

Deep–seated hatreds,
class or parent driven,
were then, are now the gauntlets.
Spoken or written words
the hands that slapped them down.
Then shame or pride
or unholy alliances line us up,
one kind against the other.
But in this sunshine which is "other" here?
That is, if both of us stay speechless.

That's better, your smile alone, without
accompanying words, says volumes.
And aren't we and both our smiles
far more alike than not?
Sometimes (as much as I love words,
which are the fair and foul extension
of our thoughts) I cannot help but wish
we'd all of us been born without our tongues.

Anti–War

Peace Pentecost
1981

Mr. Sam Williams, you run a neat and tidy plant —
Snow white, grass green —
But I recognize the bleached bones
and the stinking flesh
inside your whited sepulchers.

We blew balloons with hope
and tied them to your nice, clean fence.
I didn't have a string
so I used a bandaid from my pocket.
We prayed that the Holy Spirit would fill you
as we filled those bright balloons.

Do you realize that your guards,
neat, uniformed, erect, efficient,
so quick to undo our efforts,
without a speck of color left
to litter up that broad expanse of lawn,
have loosed our breath and spirit on your world?

Spring 1988

There's going to be a dearth of maple trees,
judging by the wealth of squawkers
cluttering up the lawns and gutters of this spring.

My mother used to say much the same of baby boys
when born in disproportionate numbers to the girls.
"There's going to be a war," she'd say.

And of the squawkers, will some get hidden safely
underground and hold strong to their promise
till long after Fermi's killed their kind above?

Five grandchildren born these past six years,
and four of them are boys. God grant quite false
these old wives' tales of baby boys and maple trees!

Special Service Confusion

Whose keeper did you say I was?
And does my brother want my keeping?
Don't I bring him Coke, and a vinyl coat?
Don't I sell him arms to kill his neighbor?
How many light bulbs equal one life
in a tent or a cave or a one–room shack?
There's something gone so amiss in the air
and in the yards and yards of that fabric
of red–white–and–blue that we form into
the very fabric of our lives, and of theirs.
My brother crouches like an ant under the
threat of my boot. When I step on him,
and on his myriad relatives, I hardly
look down or take notice of this trivia.

They say there are more ants
than any other living thing.

Gulf War Fatality

She would remember
what she'd been doing on that day
when her illusions smashed brittle
and washed down the sink tidily,
when her ears shattered to the riotous
shouts of U! S! A!
and her heart at last burst beyond hug–mending.

She'd been rolling out cookie dough.
Her small grandson's eager little floury face,
nothing but a never–to–bloom bud of a face,
his tiny innocent hand poised with a dinosaur cutter,
suddenly raised questioning eyes to her sharp silence.

Over his head she'd seen the fat TV general,
nintendo, prime–time–live game general,
and the masses of retreating children
(who left but children after eight years
draining men in their own fool's war?),
sitting ducks in the carnival gallery
we've all been trained to, immune to.
TV general, pointer in hand, pseudo–teacher,
sounding proud to his own attempted laughter.

She would remember
her mind had heard that same laughing before,
laughing of U! S! A! in the picture
of Chief Big Foot at Wounded Knee in the snow;
but her ears hadn't been tuned to the transfer.

She would remember
when the goose–stepping, the horsed troops in blue,
the air aces, and the fresh–faced girls in the tanks
all blended to one moving mass against life;
but her heart would not make the connection.

She would remember
the laughing in the U! S! A! chants
merging with mobs of half–sheathed faces,
mobs wild open mouths chanting "Ayatollah!"
All senses knew suddenly, remembered fully
until her ears and her heart slammed her eyes shut.

The puzzle pieces were all accounted for now,
before the TV general wrote a book,
pretending no malice destroying water for oil,
pretending they weren't children bombed in retreat;
hypnotic chants growing faint, but still proud.

Her mind crashed through the tight–squeezed eyes,
to defy him at the heart of his pride.
But she could see one grain of honesty gained:
the horror of war can't be swept under the carpet
when we all know that the carpet is bomb.

The puzzle pieces were all around her now,
back, to the sides, to the front pressing in,
suffocatingly close, they grabbed and caught her up
in one last huge swirl of pain, then formed
the strait–jacket for her dear sweet welcome madness,
when she would remember no more.

Forever and Ever?

Where does it end, the marketplace?
The farmer whose staple was beans
gets his beans from a can
and his tortillas already formed.

How far have we come?
And in which direction?
How to know the "Pearl of great price"
when the oyster is seeded,
or when the plastic looks
just like the genuine?

When we wage nuclear war
(with depleted uranium arms,
nice, sound commercial touch)
for the oil to make plastics
so the masses may buy fake pearls?

When the nightmare of that war
stretches to child–killing blockades?
Eleven years after our "smart" bombs
the victor refuses to show mercy;
and our prayers rise from us just
to only our Blessed Economy.

Is it now, must it always be,
Agora aeternam, Amen?

The Ununited Front

This government does not reflect this people.
Why was the corporate media surprised,
after that awful event, that this people
behaved so heroically? As a good people will,
they pulled out all the plugs in an effort
to save, to help, and to try to console.

The people responded with caring and love.
The government responded with a vengeance!

Those at the top say they think that they know
why so much of the world seems to hate us so.
Throwing out words like 'jealous', 'civilization',
and 'freedom', they make light excuses. They
don't care which catch–phrases they bandy about
as long as they shout out from that so–called
high moral ground, and the people not question.

But the real money still goes to the pentagon,
and the pentagon still plots more destruction.
And so bitterness in the bent minds increases,
as our people weep at this sad war's destruction,
and wonder why the U.S. in government
will not try to represent US.

A Crucifixion

The crazy lady wore hotpink pants
and carried a six volt flashlight.
She could have been somebody's grandmother
or some homeless schizo off the streets.
When first arrested, she shone her light
into the darkest corners of the cells,
and the roaches and the rats sitting at their
bright–lit desks were caused to run for cover.

The officials went to their official writers, crying,
"Real light's no good at all for our wealth–health,
but the damned word carries such weight
with the mobs when we give a speech.
Better invent us a new word, or else do what
you're really good at, the double entendre —
now Peacekeeper, that was a gem!
There just must be some dark dirty word for light.
Just don't let her shine that real light again.
It hurts; it's not cost–effective,
and the mobs out there could get ideas.

The crazy lady came of age at sixty–five,
and the thought of a dole for silence made her vomit.
She'd already tried chaining herself
to the fence in front of the bomb factory.
(six hundred, sixty–five bucks to forget about bombs)
The police had simply cut through the chain.
So she thought, and she planned, and this time she forged.
A friend helped her weld steel bands
round arms and legs, neck and torso
till she fit the fence like a glove.
In the cool of the dawn as they came for her,
she drew warmth from the burning of the cards
double–talked Medicare and Social Security.

They took away her six volt.
They cried out their writers' poor efforts,
like "We are the dark, and the Darkness
will gain you sweet bondage";

but the mobs kept on coming in waves.
All in the mobs carried six volts
and hammers, and crowbars and voices
of righteous indignation, all the while singing,
"This place needs more light in!"
Together with speed and harmony and brick–by–brick
they dismantled the factory and exposed it.

The crazy lady's dazzling smile then
cut to the hearts of the troopers.
And one cried, "Let me take her out,
for she's the cause of this whole mess!"
But the mobs made a human circle
around her and her piece of forged fence.
Her smile's light pierced through the gray,
and her laugh struck bright sparks in the cold.
Then the trooper boss called off his men.
"No! We can't make a martyr here.
Killing or wounding a loony
won't come off so good in the press.
Now put up your guns, and cool heads, everyone."

But the governor himself had flown in by copter.
They could have their reactors, have their bombs
(keeping them decently hidden, of course).
Only thing we can't have here is anarchy.

He grabbed for a trooper's revolver.
The crazy lady's sweet laugh was cut off,
as her blood fell on her hotpink pants
and nourished her link in The Chain.

I Do Not Fear What You Will Do To Me

I do not fear what you will do to me
    without your guns —
You've never even offered that as option —
But with them, I am always at your mercy,
a mercy you may give just any name you choose,
    like Freedom
    like Democracy
    like Free Trade
    or even Self–Sufficiency.
Your guns may be even deadlier
    shooting dollars.

To Gaea
September, 2001

O tough and gentle mother earth, earth goddess,
I'm charmed first by your beauty, then your age.
You've seen all the evil man can work against you,
yet never failed to bring forth young in spring
or call us home when we are tired to death.

Did you affect Adam so?
(or whoever was the first to walk your soil?)
Were his eyes stung with joy
the first time he beheld your wonders?
Did you give and give to his insatiable wants,
then give again when he was turned out
away from his first perfect home?

When I thrust my hands into the surface
of your being to plant your seeds of life,
I feel your pulse, your inexhaustible patience with us.
For the love of you, if not of God,
help us to survive with you,
as you surely will survive without us.
Please help us to ride out this present storm.

To Mr. Bush, Et Al, In Lieu of War

"War is hell," the wise men say
Yet, being men, they wage it.
I can think of countless ways
to spend testosterone than that.

Fund a scientist who will find a cure
for blood lust. Or wear an estrogen patch.

Beget a better generation with your raging sex,
and mend your women's hearts with love.

Care for your children in a "kinder, gentler" way,
a way your fathers obviously did not.

Bury your dead. Confess where you've been wrong.
Be man enough to call your enemy "brother".

Take up books, not arms, the next time out,
to learn from history before you set out to repeat it.

Rebuild those ugly heaps of rubble–world
last caused by bomb and sneak attack.

Stop lying! Now there's a noble, manly cause.
Hard to break your habit of it. Will take real work.

Make what you are match what you profess.
Stop waving flags; it wastes your energy for hugging.

And this is just my short list.

First Response
Nine–One–One

Perhaps more than hatred called out that day.
Maybe the whole world screamed, "Help!"
After trying to get the Power's attention,
tell it something was so wrong with our
System's systems, it cried out with a
crude desperation. We rule by force and not law,
so we must understand this forceful display.

What the Powers heard on that infamous day
was a threat to its own extravagant ways,
(which they chose, of course, to call 'freedom').
The Power's response was to run and hide out,
lest it be called on to answer for what it did,
failed to do, then swaggered back out to wage war,
but a war on the dust of the hopeless.

What chances were missed when the S O S sounded,
and we rock with the shock of it still.
The military, so glutted, gets beefed up the more,
as we brag to our allies we'll go it alone,
and damn those who dare tell us we're wrong!
We've stated the terms: either with or against us;
but forget that they've nothing to lose. If it's
big bombs or starvation, they may yet eat our dust.

The Poor Man's War

O Come with me and let's celebrate
The perfect poor man's war.
We pay for it; we die in it
like it never was before.
While the rich who sit astride our backs
(and we all know who they are)
have writ the laws that keep them out
of this, the Poor Man's War.

But you've gotta be better than working poor,
and don't you ever forget it,
not too poor to pay those taxes
if you expect to get any credit.
This war can't happen without our help.
Do we know what Powers we are?
We slave away, their bills to pay
for this, the Poor Man's War.

For those who are too dumb to work
or fight (or won't learn the knack),
the feds would as lief lock up the lot
just to keep 'em off its back.
They pull the poor folks off the aid
that kept the wolf from their door,
claiming we can't afford it now.
(if they're not fodder for the Poor Man's War.)

"But please buy those cars that guzzle
the fuel we've deemed worth killing for."
It's for oil and wealth, and not our health,
that we wage the Poor Man's War.
And the other side? Why, they don't count!
Who's counting? And what for?
We just put 'em out of their misery
when we fight the Poor Man's War.

Now those who fight are not the rich sons
of bin Ladens or Cheneys or Bushes.
Their boys hide away, safe from the fray,
lest some missile should graze the tushes
of scions of the rich, first in patriot's hearts.
Ah, statesmen all, and true leaders.
(But keep in mind how they rob us blind,
that whole bunch of bottom–feeders!)

But you! You can be big heroes, man,
and your families all can brag.
And if you get killed, your Uncle Sam
will give all your widows a flag.
Still, if your job is spraying the Round Up,
and then your health runs out of luck,
don't look to Washington for some help;
don't imagine that they'll give a fuck!

In future years they'll all sing of you,
when all the war's stories are told,
how you bled and died and killed and cried
for those rich oil folk's long oily road.
But wait. Somethin' here's not quite right.
We've been down this same road before.
How could we have been so used again?
Every war is The Poor Man's War.

Worry

After Bush's "Nuclear Posture" Slip

Withhold, withheld, withholding
Evil knowledge from the public.
Deprivations, lamentations,
Calling out with tears
For what we ever long for,
A future without fears,

And solace for the heart.

Comfort, comforted, comforting,
Just the mother's stock in trade,
Crooning, holding, wrapped in sorrow,
Wondering if the madmen at the helm
Will give her children a tomorrow.

Die, dead, death and dying,
Too soon even for those madmen
Not convinced yet of the wonder
And the magic that life holds.
Pray, prayed over, praying,
That those who love to study war
Will learn what love is really for,
And that only peace is gold,
That they'll listen to their conscience,

Then choose the better part.

Children of Man

I'd thought that only my sons were smart.
They alone made me proud.
Just their smiles tugged my heart.

I believed that only my daughters were pretty.
They were perfectly formed.
They were wise. They were witty.

I'd never once seen such children as mine.
None on earth so fair,
none on earth so fine.

Then the government called my children to war,
to learn to hate, and then murder
mothers' children they'd not seen before.

I knew then that all mothers' sons are smart.
All sons are dear to their own mother's heart.
All daughters of mothers are both sweet and pretty.
All daughters are perfect and perfectly witty.

It's easy to say it's the government's war,
that it makes us kill those we've not seen before;
but the lesson to learn, if learn it we will,
is all children of all mothers must learn not to kill.

Each

I make no claim but hope.
I have no tool but wanting.
But I walk beneath no one's banner but my own;
I only choose to disclaim yours
if you pull me under it with you.

Insistent voices, inner ones from past times,
Call out brash contrasts that offer
nothing really, while they try to tempt with all.

Thou shalts and thou shalt nots from millennia ago,
misunderstood, yet parroted for centuries
by those who taught me and who taught my teachers' teachers,
would shove me into drawers where I do not fit
and put me in boxes whose lids will not stay on.

Not a rebel, not a revolutionary, I,
but simply one who will no longer join your army,
fight your wars, or mold me to match your cause.
And I give you and the whole world notice
that any rallying slogan I repeat from now
must be true on all the sides of it,
or I will denounce it publicly,
then teach others they don't have to join up for the joining.

Golden Years

(with apologies to Perry Como, et al)

Unlucky, unlucky, unlucky me.
I'm an unlucky son–of–a–gun.
I eat eight hours,
so I sleep eight hours,
then I worry eight hours for fun.

Unlucky, unlucky, unlucky me.
When my story truly is spun,
I read eight hours,
then I write eight hours
till my eyes have come undone.

> I don't mean to deplore
> or assume to ignore
> all the crafts to which
> seniors are prone.

> I'd like to crochet,
> but I can't find a way
> with the world in this
> nuclear zone.

Unlucky, unlucky, unlucky me.
Doomed to read, write, work, worry, and pray
that the news won't be bad,
that the saints won't be had,
that we won't blow our world away.

Hopeless

When the Sierra Club and the Wilderness Society
pictures seem to be so much easier to find
and so much better than the real thing —
When your bored and only comment
when you view the giant redwood is:
Let's go. I've seen this shot before —

When you begin to marvel
with those tired–out old–timers about
the wondrous three–tiered expressways —
and never mind the damned expressway's
replaced and dumped huge tons of concrete
on an ecofield of daisies —

When the trickling, purple flower–bordered,
three–inch–high cataract up Mount Hood's side
is simply mud beneath your boot —
When a crusted, jeweled, ice–and–snow
creation, filigreed onto an evergreen
means just: I hope this thaws by noon —

Then you, my child, are hopeless.
Needn't worry on Caesar's taxes, or a Sanctuary worker,
or a Trident, or a Star War, 'cause you're through.

The Protester

She didn't choose them —
fluffy curtains, flowery paper.
Were she in charge,
she'd have picked just room–darkening shades
and clean matte paint.

He lived in other people's homes by day,
took up their tastes.
The rich who could afford to have him
turn their bedrooms all to flowery fluff
taught him their lines and colors,
and he never asked if she'd have liked it different.

You ask why she chose prison
(I mean besides her obvious protest of this war);
perhaps she simply felt the need of
other than Republican decor.

Little Dove

Miranda is so tender–hearted
she won't step on a flower in her way.
When told of the infamous tower–attack,
of the pain, suffering and terror born on that day,

she said, "Don't kill 'em back."

She sees what so many adults will not see,
adults lined up and ready to join in the fray:
she knows that killing will never stop killing.
Instead, it just drives us the opposite way.

She says, "Don't kill 'em back."

Only one woman in Congress could see
that more terror just helps spread more terror.
The President, Congress, many citizens too,
still cannot admit to their error,

but Miranda says, "Don't kill 'em back."

Three religions are met on a battlefield there,
deciding if life for us all will go on.
Three peoples of the Book, who won't heed what it teaches,
still insist on their vain warathon,

while Miranda says, "Don't kill 'em back.

Miranda, who's seven, already knows
that life is too precious to end it,
or to order it killed, as our government does,
while pretending to seek to defend it.

And Miranda says' "Don't kill 'em back."

We extend our cruel wars in her father's homeland.
Colombia's people are under our attack.
We kill off the crops, kill the flowers, kill the LIFE,

yet Miranda pleads, "Don't kill 'em back."

Anti–War

Tickle Your Funny Bone

Mud Song

Slipping around in the mud is fun,
Oozing it up 'twixt my toes.
The very best part of a rainstorm is this:
The mud that it leaves when it goes.

If Mom would just try it this once for herself,
'Stead of screaming, "Get out of that crud!",
She'd find nothing can tickle your funny bone quite
Like slipping around in the mud.

Forecast: Drifting

I walked a path of downy snow,
this lovely June sixth morning.
I guess the weatherman didn't know;
it came without a warning.

I kicked the fluffy stuff about.
I'd had no way of knowing
when I'd got dressed and stepped outside
that the cottonwoods were blowing!

Homecoming

I've been gone for hours too long.
He sits by the window in anticipation.
As soon as my key is turned
and I've pushed wide the door,
he leaps into my arms.

He smothers my arms and neck
and then my face with scratchy kisses.
When I sit down, he snuggles up
close to me, his contented sighs
telling me louder than words
that my cat has missed me.

Communication

Checkov had ways of
getting what he wanted.
He whined. He wheedled.
Sometimes he threw himself at her.
He'd wait until she started to read,
then slyly bite her newspaper
out of her hands and onto the floor.
He'd fling himself at her neck
(he knew her weaknesses),
and kiss her in frantic passion.

But when he really knew
that he must leave her,
then he'd just bark
once.

First Step

I cannot wake
At some far date
And find the world improved.
I cannot make
Perfection or mistake
Without my having moved.

Miracles are fine,
A poor man's panacea.
Faith devout
Has helped us mortals out
Through years of near–despair.

But
        The person I will be,
        The world I will see,
        The changes so profound,
        The gaining of the ground,
        The rising from despair,
        And the washing of that stack of dishes there:
These all depend on me.

Amish or Not, Here It Goes

Enough! I say then of our friendship
and this delectable Friendship Cake!
Thousands of calories overtake me
with each sweet loaf that I bake.
Some "friendship", indeed, is that
bent on making me more fat.
Were you here now, I would shake

you, and my peers would me defend;
for every time I eat one up,
I've saved the starter in a cup.
Then once more I mix to make me stout.
That's it! I'll throw the damned thing out!
This Cake–Friendship's at an end!

Getting Even

I was glad the rain came
putting out the fires
of all those who burned their leaves
and my throat and eyes.

I found me wishing
it would rain for months
so they could never burn
(though the molds produced
would certainly hurt my breathing).

Spite my face!
It was revenge time now,
and I wanted rain
because I knew they didn't.

Anyone who lights up
mounds of leaves in an air inversion
(or any time),
I thought, deserves to be rained upon
until they build an ark!

Clean–Up Squads

It is easy to think
what you would do
after long decades spent
with my clutter
of books and papers:
A huge mountain
of black plastic bags
by the curb
in the morning.

And I — I would dig
a big hole out back,
take your gun and
your TV out there,
shoot one,
and then bury them both.

Deadlines

My sister explained the three "olds"
as our mother lay ill:
there was the young old, which we both were;
there was the old old, which was our mother;
and, somewhere between, there was a medium old.

I've always needed deadlines —
never sorted out the word, just knew
that pressures of a time near–up were
motivation enough. The assignments,
written on the eves of dates I'd known
about for weeks; the housecleaning,
frantically done an hour ahead of guests;
the mailing in of bills due, never late,
but post–marked to be barely "on" and not "before."

But nothing had prepared this
procrastination–vet for this: the very real
and unadorned death–deadline
that made itself felt now I've reached
my medium old. It's Redd Foxx's "Big One".
Finale. Fini. Last and final put–off.

And how I plan to fine–tune the thing,
hone my life–long talent to perfection,
plan a veritable career, pursue a doctorate,
in short (but LONG!) spend every hour
of every day of all the months and years
I'm given actively, assiduously putting off!

Who's the Cook Here, Anyway

"This chicken is horribly tough," you said,
And I certainly won't say that you lied,
But you never once tell me the chicken is tough
When I serve you Kentucky Fried.

"I like your home–cooking the best, my girl,"
Still you roared like a towering inferno
That my dough was decidedly doughy; and yet
You just smile when I give you DiGiorno.

"These biscuits are light as a feather, My Love,"
You once said, and it filled me with joy
Until I remembered I'd run out of flour —
You were praising the Pillsbury Dough Boy.

I know a way, though, to encourage your taste
So you'll blubber that everything's fine:
I'll pour you before every meal you ingest
Several glasses of my home–made wine.

August Daze

What is so rare as a male mosquito,
Even one traveling incognito.
And what is worse, (here the chance gets rarer)
You can't even find 'em in a male–female pair.

The mama always says without introduction
That she needs your blood, or the species' destruction
Will be on your head (while the papa plays dead,
Or stays out–of–sight); and she picks your ear first
To try to appease her unquenchable thirst.

So the gist of this verse, and the point of this tale:
I've set neither eyes nor ears
On a mosquito who's male.

Moves of Water

It should be a canon of law
and of faith
that each must spend
a whole day or night
alone with water.

A river as it laps
white water as it laughs aloud
or drops far distances in foam
eternal water as it tides in and out
beach water wave upon wave

Lacking these,
a night spent with the constant drip
of a leaking faucet
will also humble and amaze.

Quawx Blidho Supyy

Well, I'll be jabberwocked!
I've found your technique, Carroll.
Now remember, I'm your fan
but I could no more understand
those words of yours I love than fly.

But watch me soar now that I've
found your method out.
Like seeing in a blinding light
a rare brushstroke of Matisse,
the riddle of your Seussian words I've bested:
In the great Word Search of Life
you chose to choose
only the words not listed!

Some Common Ordinary Questions

Is effect causative,
or cause effective?
I hover under the very edge
of kenning what knowledge births
and what begets the knowing.
Caught out upon a ledge
of wondering what is sensual
and a sensing of the wondrous.

Perhaps if I can span the rational,
I can rationalize the spanning
of this place I cross,
then step lighter because of
that Light to which my steps must lead.

The Doctor Is In (and taking a nap)

Are cats our consciences,
Worrying over the fitness of our souls?
I sense in those bright eyes
that they would pardon every sin I could confess.

They cannot fathom all my foolishness,
cannot ken my inability to rest,
just don't get why I'm obsessed with things.

"Relax," I almost hear the purring voice —
psychiatrist or priest —

"Lean back now. Close those tired eyes.
Just let someone else take over now, and sleep."

To D.L. on the Windowsill

O inscrutable cat,
would you rather not be where you're at?
Would you rather be skinny, not fat?

Is your mysterious soul not at rest?
Would that free life outdoors be the best?
Did your people here fail your mute test?

Have we captured you whole
in your pet enforced–role?
At that window, is freedom your goal?

Do you wish mites and fleas were still there?
That you chased a live mouse everywhere?
Do you miss all those burs in your hair?

When you munch and you crunch on your lunch,
are you fed up with the whole human bunch?
Or (as always with you), do I not have a hunch?

Dilemma

I identify with the working class,
and the working class is me.
And so I could never pay anyone
to do the things that I ought to do,
    but feel too tired to do,
    or can afford not to do,
    or I'm sick of doing

'cause that would identify me
as part of the woes of the working class.
I'd be the manager man, the bossy man,
the never–get–her–hands–dirty queen
who were always too rich or too mean
to care for the likes of me.

So I struggle along and hate the rich;
and I'm tired and bent and old,
and sick to the death of the work I do.
And I'm ready to crack and fold.

Still, I'll be damned if I'll be the boss,
the manager, Lord, or king.
For how could I hold my contempt intact
if I met him and he was me?

Fallings

Fallings're
more desirable than droppings.
Fallings can be
better than the risings.
But not if it's a cake you're baking.
Fallings, if you're buying, and it's cost, it's
better, but worse if you're the seller.
Fallings're
lots of fun if snow's it,
but full of fear if you're it.
Fallings're
great if it's in love you're,
but from a building, no way!
Still, off a bridge and bungied, fun.
Fallings're
thrilling on a roller–coaster,
chilling in an airplane,
but as a babe to Daddy's arms
a fine game and secure.
Fallings're
sad when flower petals do it,
but, if tears, yet you are smiling, fine.

Time's Up

I used to count my time well–spent
when one thing got complete:
The dishes done, a lesson planned,
A meal made, fit to eat.

I used to think I'd done so well
If all I'd done at all
Was think upon God's Being,
Or love, one day in fall.

I used to know tomorrow'd come
When I could finish up
Whatever thing I'd started on
To fill an empty cup.

I used to trust the day would come
I'd look and see me done
With every stupid household chore:
Then I could just have fun.

I used to… aah, but what's the use
To think on used–to's now?
I don't have time or sweet ambition
Or even pure know–how.

All these things unfinished —
I haven't got the time
To be, to do, to think, to make —
Even this silly rhyme.

Spring and Other Fevers

My body knows its own canonical year:
May first — time for early grasses and weeds
First frost — end of ragweed and late weeds.

The dusts and mites,
The cat and dog and horse
(danders, furs, salivas),
The feathers
All injected weekly round the calendar.

The molds (largest vials most vile!)
Used most in summer, spring and fall,
Tapering off in winter.

I don't have to see my modern watch
For a hundred sneezes in a row
To tell me Monday's here, Injection Day

I don't need to look out the window
To hear my stuffed head,
My gritty eyes
My nose spigot running free
Calling to me
   "The pollens are coming!
   The pollens are coming!"

I'd gladly trade you, even up,
Your signs of spring for mine.

We Are Everywhere

At the end of my dust mop as I shake it:
    that's us
Flying away on the breeze.
In the vac bag crammed so tight with
    all sorts of dust,
I see us as I change it, feel us as I sneeze.
In all of that dust which we daily slough off
You might find us if only you look;
Though we've not found a way to extract
    who we were
From this dust–flaking memory book.

Not quite as pleasing, I admit that it's true,
As a photograph, relic or letter,
Still, collect all our dust of the past
    seven years,
And that's us, younger and, just maybe, better.
From the lot of it we might knit a sweater!

R.I.P.

We know pretty well that we're put here to work;
we just can't turn our backs and say, "Fudge!"
But I'm here to tell you that some jobs just ain't fair,
'cause a woman is more than a drudge.

> "Clean it up
> Pick it up
> Wash it up
> Fix it up
> Mend it up
> Serve it up
> And HURRY it up!"

And no one (not you) seems to know when you're done,
but just expect it to happen again.
I say we all laugh as though we're havin' fun,
and then share these good times with our men!

I don't think I'd shirk
if I could pick my own work.
I think then I would do my fair share.
Let my tombstone declare
(whatever causes I've espoused):
"This woman wasn't no wife to no house!"

Lost Cause

Each spring I plan to be
a "lady" gardener.
(My mother had hands,
soft, smooth and white.)
I buy the seedling flats,
gloves at the ready,
gloat those first few days
about my spotless hands.

I begin to clip and trim
without a blister,
fill up the hanging pots,
stand back to admire.
But then, somehow,
when weeding starts,
the itch to feel the earth
nudges at me. I cannot
know weeds' stubborn roots
without I touch them.
I cannot breathe the earth
without my skin.

At first one glove is off,
then I put by the other.
I'm hopeless. I can never be
a gardener like my mother.

On the Move

I moved vicariously
through my children
through the years
west
northwest
east
further east
southwest
northeast

saving the letters
precious
sometimes in body
visiting
always visiting
in mind
heart, each time,
part of the moves

while my very own
moves
were extravagant
and varied too:
north (one house)
south (half a mile)
three homes on this
same rural road

Out of Like

Did love blind us at the time
we vowed we'd always stay sublime?
How can I say this, dear,
except I really, truly fear
I've fallen out of like with you.

For we don't like the same friends;
we don't like the same films;
can't really stomach the same sort of food.

I can't stand your subtle humor,
your belief in things that I call rumor,
and you think my jokes are coarse and rude.

You say my music's just plain weird;
I love the rhythms you call queer,
(not to mention, dear, the fact of your tin ear).

Add toilet seats and toothpaste lids
to put this marriage on the skids,
and the list goes on and on and on, I fear.

For we don't like the same pets;
we don't like the same pillow,
don't even like the same side of the bed.

How can we go ahead this way
and find more differences each day?
Can't we steer another course instead?

But divorce just wouldn't do it;
that can't be the answer to it.
Though liking one another seems a curse,
I believe if we should try it,
we might find (now don't deny it)
We could each get stuck with someone who is worse.

Mea Culpa, Vegetarians

Oh the pure joy and sweet pleasure of fresh pickled pigs feet!
Served up on rusk they're a true palate's rare treat.
Whether you are a deadbeat or a social elite,
you'll feel right at home eating pickled pigs feet.

To me they're much better than pancakes of buckwheat
or that Russian soup, borsch, that is made from the red beet.
They're the very best kind of all kinds of pigmeat,
these luscious and scrumptious tidbits of pigs feet.

Some like them broiled on a fire of mesquite.
Some like them spiced hot, while some take them plain neat.
But there's nothing compares to a meal that's complete
with some jellied and juicy and tender pigs feet.

If you're cooking some up, I'll be there in a heartbeat.
Or I'll ask you out here if you promise to help eat
(whether home–grown or sent here from far away Crete)
some wonderful, fanciful, flavourful pigs feet.

You could take loin and apples and mix up some mincemeat,
but for eating that's old and yet so new and upbeat
I guarantee if you eat, you will leave here replete
with your tummy stuffed full of these yummy pigs feet.

April Confession

I seek the asparagus, mouth awash
with anticipatory relish, all along those
rocky slant sides of the old tracks.
Furtively I look about, like the
gold prospector that I am,
anxious only to protect my claim.

Then it is with the gentle steaming
and the application of some butter
drizzled lightly over the freshness
that the Gift Royal (or at least the
triumphant celebration of my theft)
is put on the table with no need of
garnish or particular arrangement.
This spring booty has been mine
in long winter contemplation.
I sit me down to feast.

I give no thought, no attempt made now
to hide my guilt. I couldn't if I chose.
I'd tell you outright if you asked;
for within an hour of consumption
my pee reeks of my stealthy deed.

To a Man's Heart

She woks in beauty
as the bok choy sizzles
and the napa limps
alongside the sweet red peppers.

Now the slim stalks of carrots
gentled in the warm soft sesame oil
curl round about the tiny flowering kale
whispering to the wee sweet
pods of baby peas.

He would follow anywhere she woks
because smells of succulent spicy
chicken and plump tender shrimp
surround her. The careful addition
of soy sauce to the whole
entices him to madness.

He loves the damp curls
on her forehead where she stands
in the steam of little chunks of beef,
dropping with her delicious fingers
some slithered pork into the popping oil.

He puts his arms around her waist now
as she woks, nuzzles at her neck
where the tantalizing odors of the feast
perfume her hair. He can not wait!

She piles mounds of brown rice
upon his plate, then heaps upon this
the fragrant juicy rewards of her woking.
Fit for a king!
And he would make his woker Queen.

Spring At Last

Because I am grossly short for my weight,
or very short for my gross weight,
the petite–length clam diggers
sag over the tops of my shoes
and become merely baggy pants to work in.
Oh well, I don't dig clams.

It's the lazy start–up of the spring
I know too well will be brief that speeds
me into the garden at all before the
90's come to send me off to fans and ice.
But now the rich black mud and aged manure
collect beneath my fingernails,
and there is no wall between the birds and me.

Here I am time–stopped, shutter speed: 2000,
focus: infinity in these all too few days
when global warming hasn't yet begun
to harp at my conscience; and I can
transplant the hydrangea and clip away
the old stalks of the shastas I'd neglected.

First tiny leaves spring skyward on the maples,
while the old walnut trees, in habitual fear,
hold off for zero–risk. I smile back at the
forsythias near the driveway, then watch
house finches summon all their kin
to eat at our dependable feeder.

It all looks so normal, and it may yet be
that normal looks are all I can depend on;
so I'm falling for it.

Marriage

You're sweet.
Let me warm your cold feet
on mine.
You'll be fine.
They're like ice!
but it feels kinda nice
'cause I'm tough.
Is one blanket enough?
What's that?
Did you put out the cat?
What a din!
Did you let the dog in?
Who's there?
There's a noise on the stair!
Now what?
Is the hall window shut?
Is that rain?
No, don't get up again.
I snore?
I think someone's at the door.
It's all right.
Please turn out the light.
Just sleep.
Don't you think that can keep?
A drink?
You just had one, I think.
You're back.
Well, it's hard to keep track.
You're sweet.
Let me warm your cold feet
on mine.
You'll be fine…

Computer Mind of Mine

I have been
computer–resistant.
This disease
has kept me from
understanding you
and understanding
you could cure
this, and all my illnesses.

Computer Mind of mine,
I am reprogramming
you now to give me
understanding
of your understanding.
Enough at least to let
me heal myself,
then to see myself
and my whole world anew.
Enough to give me
all your knowing
at a thought.
(or at least to give me
all that I can stand.)

Computer Mind of mine,
take all my errors
and delete them.
Lock all my caps!
Take all I am
and have been and save as.
And don't forget to
print out all my options.

Weighty Decision

Sing a song of stretch pants,
elasticized and bright.
Brushed denim for the daytime,
lush velvet for the night.
On some they look like sex–pants;
on me they're merely tight.

I love the shades they come in,
but, as I too plainly see,
regardless of the color,
what's underneath's all me.

Sing a song of stretch pants,
no room for pockets there,
no room, in fact, for anything
'twixt cloth and derriere.

When are manufacturers
ever goin' to learn:
Not every shape can stand the strain
of stretch around the stern?
With Lycra here and second–skin there,
I'm more than slightly stout.
A looser look at least might lend
the benefit of doubt.

Sing a song of stretch pants,
for fat or plump or leans,
not to mention every size
that happens in–betweens.
But I guess I'll keep on wearing
my worn–out, baggy jeans.

Mothers

My mother said
to keep me from being lazy
when I asked her why God made flies.
Then she handed me the swatter.
It really drove me crazy,
just the look in my mother's eyes.

To try to weasel out
I used my imagination
as I thought of things not to do.
The wiles that I used
drove my mother to frustration,
and I thought I'd learned a thing or two.

When my mother taught,
I had to catch her on the fly
because she worked all the live–long day
So I followed her around,
got my learning with my eyes,
helped her just to not get in her way.

But it seems her
psychology was really, really lost on me
'cause I never could get it right.
Her clever turn of phrase to make me see
what I should do just wasn't mine;
and I drove me own kids out–of–sight.

'Cause I tried it on my kids
when they told me they were bored,
thought I'd remembered my mother's ways.
I handed them a list of chores
to do to try beat their boredom;
and they kept out–of–sight for days!

Perfect Match

She was allergic to his beard.
He would not cut it off.
So when he held her tenderly,
it made her sneeze and cough.

He direly hated garlic–breath.
She was a garlic–lover.
It made his eyes stream mightily;
he felt that he would smother.

They both were stubborn in their way
about what the other hated.
She coughed and sneezed — hugged him anyway;
he kissed her with eyes irritated.

So, coughing, sneezing, teary–eyed.
They went off hand–in–hand.
Each vowed to each eternal love.
The moral: Ain't love grand?

Still She Snores

A good woman, that I'll grant you,
but she snores.
Worse than any noise extant
are her worst snores,
and there's nothing more annoring
than her snoring.
I jamb my pillow in my ear
but she comes in loud and clear
with her snoring.
I've just got to get some sleep — it's killing.
This couch-vigil that I keep ain't thrilling.
She can be sweet as she can be
but I'm deploring
that her charms are lost to me
by that snoring.

There's no freight train ever worser
than her snores.
Ain't no cursing more accurser
than those snores.
Grab my hand before I cuff her;
with her pillow I could snuff her,
even though, God knows, I luff her,
I sure hates her snores.
I now get no sleep at all
because she snores.
Spend nights staring at the wall
and hearing snores.
Those snores so loud and limber
ain't a thing can dull the timbre
of her snores.
Ear plugs barely dim the edges
of her snores,
and I make me solemn pledges
that I won't run out of doors
next time she snores.
But when she starts again, by dammie,
I'd gladly sock her one big whammie,
Or choke her off with my pajammie
when she snores.

I had a dream that makes me shudder
when I tell.
Thought they'd put her six feet under
but her snores rose up like thunder
straight from hell.
If I go to meet my Lord
and He points low,
I'll plead mercy 'cause I been there,
this I know.
If He lets me tell my story
He'll know I done my Purgatory
with her snores.
If I die and go to Heaven,
I'll know all my sins forgiven
by the hellish life I'm livin'
with her snores.

She's a great old gal in most ways,
but she snores.
She can sleep all night and most days;
still she snores.
I sneak off to bed quite early,
welcome sleep, like gates so pearly,
but no sooner than I'm sleepin'
than her snores start in a–keepin'
me from sleep, no matter if that sleep
is light or deep, in come those snores.
Lord knows I've tried to leave her
and her snoring,
moved from room to room in vain
with sad deploring.
Let me just say, if you're a doubter,
can't sleep with her; can't sleep without her
and her snoring.

Strange Legacy

Oh, my dear Papa,
You did what you hadn't oughter!
Just because you had no sons,
Why did you give this to your daughter?

Male Pattern Baldness

I know your dad was bald,
And I know that you were too.
I know those genes are active guys,
But they could have stopped with you.

Male Pattern Baldness

There are many things you might have
Left me I'd have liked a lot,
But a bare spot on this pate of mine
I certainly do not!

Male Pattern Baldness

Chemicals, potions, lotions,
Weird transplants, surgery,
Lies, laser, strange oils, quackery,
Vows, promises, and a guarantee —
This stuff just ain't for me.

I'll keep my Male Pattern Baldness

And I won't wear a wig or flip.
I think they're just as bad.
I'll grin and bear, and proudly swear
I'm out to start a fad.
If I hear any rude remarks, I'll smile,
"Yes, my sweet gift from my sweet Dad!"

Male Pattern Baldness

MY Male Pattern Baldness!

Tickle Your Funny Bo

Is It Just Me?

(Or Just an Example of the
Shirley M. Steinman Theory of
Time–Speed Relativity at Work?)

It's always a quarter to five,
and I always must go start some dinner.
No matter how early or late I arrive;
or even, perchance, if we have just et,
and I've not even done up those last dishes yet,
still it's always a quarter to five.
It's no wonder that I can't get thinner.

I'm late just as soon as I wake,
though of rest not one second I take;
for no matter the time by the sun when I start,
I first check my watch and then grab at my heart —
for it's always a quarter to five.

This time warp I'm in is some jive:
if I start or I stop or I stay just the same,
Time's insistent on playing its frustrating game
of being a quarter to five.

Perhaps I am under some spell
that was cast on me when I turned 60.
I'll put up a sign, so Time knows very well:
"Time, if you breakie, you fixie!"

I'm not saying you'll turn out like me,
but, by way of a caution, I plea:
If you plan to grow older, and want to survive,
wait 'til after a quarter to five.

Colophon

Book and cover design by Jan Steinman, using Adobe InDesign® and Photoshop® on Apple Macintosh® computers. The body font is ITC Souvenir. The title font is John Doe, by Ethan Dunham. The cover photo is a selection of my Mom's favorite poems that she wrote down on index cards and gave to me. The back cover photo is from August 1985, overlooking the Central Oregon Cascade Mountains.